OU!

TURN FE[AR] INTO JOY

PRACTICE

[CHA]LLE[N]GE

HOW WILL YOU CHANGE the WORLD?

ON.

MOUNTAINS OF SUCCESS

FORGET THE CRYSTAL BALL

[EN]DLESS

FLY!

You ARE not alone in THIS WORLD.

YOU Can Do

BREATH ANYTHING

Pay It Forward

[H]EAL

NOBODY'S PERFECT

[S]OCIAL MEDIA

[A]PPROACH WITH CAUTION

TRANSFORM STRESS for GOOD

NO ONE IS PERFECT: DON'T JUDGE

[S]HOULDERING

THE PAIN AND THE GAIN

BECOMING A

[C]ATALYST

YOU CAN BE A SUPERHERO TOO!

UNCERTAIN ANSWERS

WOWsdom!

The girl's guide to the POSITIVE and the POSSIBLE

WOWsdom!

The girl's guide to the POSITIVE and the POSSIBLE

Share the WOW !

Donna Orender

Created by
DONNA ORENDER
FOREWORD BY GERALDINE LAYBOURNE

MASCOT® BOOKS

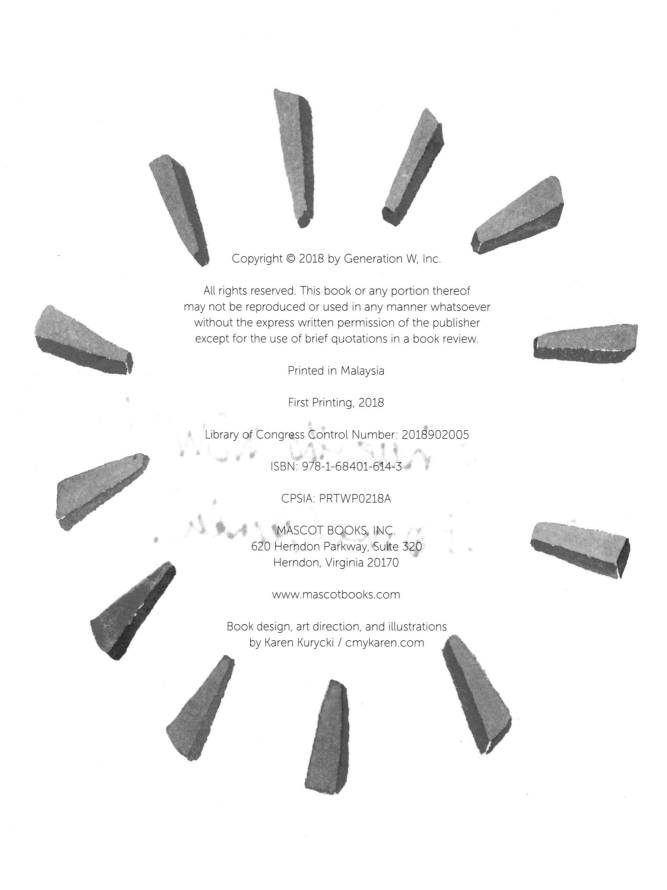

Printed in Malaysia

First Printing, 2018

Library of Congress Control Number: 2018902005

ISBN: 978-1-68401-614-3

CPSIA: PRTWP0218A

MASCOT BOOKS, INC.
620 Herndon Parkway, Suite 320
Herndon, Virginia 20170

www.mascotbooks.com

Book design, art direction, and illustrations
by Karen Kurycki / cmykaren.com

DEDICATION

To the angels within us that yearn to fly.

For young girls everywhere—
may you sing the songs of your hearts as loudly as you please.

Thanks, Mom and Dad, for believing that girls can do anything
and for sharing that message with me and my sisters.

And to my angel, MG, who knows that women can do everything and wouldn't have it any other way.
To him and the family we have raised, my unending devotion and love.

CONTENTS

THE POSSIBLE
THE POSITIVE
YOUR PASSION
PURPOSE

FOREWORD

by Geraldine Laybourne

Welcome to the Donna Orender Orbit. I guess I need to explain that: **Donna loves ideas and people, especially X-chromosomed people.** She starts with an inspiring idea, gathers everyone she knows who would both learn and teach others, and she ignites the exchange. She's touched the lives of thousands of women and girls, building community, inclusive of all, wherever she goes. **WOWsdom!** extends the orbit to you.

You're going to have fun with this interactive book. **WOWsdom!** is filled with very personal stories from a wide variety of leaders in the form of advice to our younger (or, in some case, future) selves. It was a crazy process for the contributors: we ended up remembering some of the great energy and optimism we had in our youth and ended up uncovering things to improve our lives today. And we loved thinking about what pieces of our journey you might benefit from. The young girls shared their fears, triumphs, worries, and nuggets for success. I love thinking about what their future—and YOURS—holds.

The Orender Orbit works like this: once you're in it, you come away richer with inspiration, ideas, and new friends. A few years ago, at her Generation W event, she asked me to moderate a panel with a fourteen-year-old, a 100-year-old, and a few in-betweeners. It was a toss-up of who learned more from whom. The luckiest among us got to know Donna years ago and have watched her inspire girls with everything she does. Her touch has been incredibly personal and effective. **What amazes me about this book is that it also feels incredibly personal—like a love note from Donna and tens of men and women like her.** Successful leaders in the military, education, media, and the arts; respected community volunteers and humanitarian activists; and brave entrepreneurs talk about struggles they had learning to read, dealing with abuse, their stubbornness to accept help, and overcoming social pressure.

The path you choose for your life is already there. Let WOWsdom! help you uncover it. I urge you to make this as interactive as possible: take scissors to the book if you want. Cut out things you want to think about. Or why not write a letter to your future self, seal it, and open it in 2030? As you write, pretend to be your own best friend and remind yourself of your strengths. And by the way–it's a good thing to actually to be a friend to yourself; some of us tend to be too hard on ourselves!

With love, respect, and affection,
Gerry

SAYING HI!

As you look back on your life, you need not be old, although you will always, by definition, be older, whether it be by days or even minutes. I always thought that I had a pretty good grasp on the world, until I looked back and wondered how I ever got by not knowing what I know now. I can distinctly remember writing on my desk (even though it was against the rules) in Ms. DiBello's eighth grade class, and I was moved in that moment to write in pencil the time, the date, and a note that this moment in time was worth remembering. I felt aware and present, and I knew that it was just a blink before it would pass. I remember writing a letter to my sixteen-year-old self from my sixteen-year-old self about what my world was like, so that I would remember what was important to me and just how strongly I felt about what was important.

I felt for certain that people just did not take a sixteen-year-old girl seriously enough.

I recall hitting thirty and wondering, "How did I ever get through my twenties without the knowledge that I had gained that brought me to the ripe old age of thirty?" This is a recurring thought as time travels. If I only knew then what I know now, things could have been so much easier. To know that we are not alone in this wonderful journey of life is truly a gift. Too often we think that it is only US thinking that we are not good enough, or that we are the only one who has parents who don't understand us, or that our fears are ours alone. And I wonder how I got through life with so many of the scrapes and bruises that living life can give you. Of course we do, we all do, but the real gift of age is experience and the real gift of youth is believing that every experience is new.

Many times in my life I have been asked, and I continue to be asked, what advice would you give to your younger self? I laugh out loud, not sure that my younger self would have listened to any advice. I was on this earth to burn my own trail; devil beware, I was coming. I mean seriously, who could have possibly understood me and my singularly unique thoughts, ideas, and passions? I laugh. **Oh, to have had an older me to pat me on the shoulder and whisper, "It will be ok, you don't need to worry so much."** Someone to hold my hand or place a guiding arm around my shoulder whose presence alone would help build my confidence. Someone to share a story and let me know that the sleepless nights and incredible angst was all a rite of passage and that I was not alone.

And so, how great we thought it would be to share the POSITIVE and the POSSIBLE from so many great women who have opened their hearts to share their stories. With the wisdom that comes from living life, and the WOW that is part of anticipating the wonders of life, WOWsdom! is for YOU! YOU, who may be soaring in the clouds or hiding in plain sight; YOU who truly wants to figure out the puzzle but are not sure where to turn, what to ask, and who is safe; the YOU who wants to be the best ME that you can be. With a few tips, you can be just that!

If I only knew then what I know now, things could have been so much easier.

Together we share a path on the continuum of time; we look back, some of us over many more years than others, knowing that reflection is powerful, and we look forward, knowing that our dreams and desires have the power to inspire us to reach and grow.

So we have it: the WOW of our girls and the WISDOM of our women. WOWsdom, this powerful energy of sharing, looking back, and looking forward as we fly together towards the best hopes and dreams of our amazing selves.

I hope this book becomes a trusted resource for you—a kind friend that is there to build your confidence, remind you of what is important, and motivate you to express yourself and to continue to learn.

Donna Orender

A nationally-recognized business leader, Donna Orender is the founder of Generation W, Generation WOW, and CEO of Orender Unlimited. She is a women's pro basketball pioneer and former WNBA president and is deeply passionate about elevating the voices of girls and women. You can learn more about what drives Donna by watching her TEDx Talk: Fear Not the Ask. *Watch now at wowsdom.com.*

USING THIS BOOK

Dear Sister Friends,

Today's women and girls navigate a society where implicit and explicit messages often silence their voices and power; it is no easy walk. Together, we have to create safe spaces to express ourselves. Accessing our voices of wisdom is how we make sound choices. Women must observe the world to figure out how to move through the noise of systemic adversities. We need to feed our courage to keep going and take chances. Let this book be your chocolate cake and springboard—your friend and mentor. Letters in this book come from a deep internal place where women along different life paths speak to their younger and future selves in honest and inspiring ways. **It is now your turn. Write, push, and face hard realities you may not say out loud.** Use this book as the impetus to tell your truth. Write and do the exercises to see your value. Read and listen to the letters written inside these covers and know you are not alone on your journey.

When you catch someone telling a story that looks like your own, smile or let the tears come. **These letters are hugs. Give a hug back.** Write to your younger self and make her feel seen and heard. Write to your future self and never let her forget the spark inside.

Be Creative and Be Well,
Yvette Angelique

> Yvette Angelique is a fierce advocate for young women. Her friendship and thoughtful support of Generation WOW has been a founding force in this movement. It's sister friends like HER that make the world a better place!

Learn more about Yvette Angelique on page 96.

WOWsdom TIPS:

In thinking about the **why** of this book, we knew we wanted girls to be better prepared for the adventure of life ahead. We wanted YOU to be more in the know, to help you be more aware, and ignite the desire to be curious and to love learning, the easy lessons and the hard.

Life offers us many classrooms, and we realize that some of the basic lessons of life (the essential and important ones, the simple ones that keep us healthy and safe, the ones that teach us about money and moving forward) come to us later than they should or not at all. We are here to teach you the things we wish we had known, much earlier than we came to know them.

So, throughout WOWsdom!, you will find special tips, WOWsdom! Tips, that are **WORDS OF WISDOM.**

Some of the coolest and smartest folks will teach and remind us what is good to put into our bodies and what is good to keep out, a few good exercises to do every day to keep us healthy and motivated, not to mention the importance of being aware that our mental health and our physical health are connected! How about understanding that we are about the company we keep and how your brain is positively impacted by doing things for others? This secret stash is the kind of stuff you want to know, but may not know where or who to ask. **It is HERE!**

In reading and engaging with this book, you will be inspired, become aware, and be active and proactive. This is all about the positive and the possible of WOWsdom! and the great, practical WOW tips coming your way.

Read on and you will enjoy!

The Importance of STORYTELLING

In my mind's eye, I see a little girl snuggled up in bed at the end of a day being read to as a nightly ritual that shaped my childhood. The security—a sense of place and space within which I belonged and understood—formed my beginnings in the world of storytelling. Hearing others' stories provided the lens of relational orientation while creating a foundation upon which I learned to share my story. And with each iteration of telling my story, I came to further understand who I was and who I am and paved the way for who I might become.

For you see, in the telling of your story, not only are you sharing a piece of who you are with the person listening to or reading your story, you are also creating a deeper understanding for yourself of who you are, how you have come to be, and why you see the world the way you do.

If you allow yourself to reflect, to really think about the story you are telling at any given point in time, you keenly uncover assumptions you have constructed. Assumptions of who you are as a person, a girl, a woman, a learner, a partner, a friend...so many pieces of the mosaic that create you, the human being.

ta nce

ELLING

These assumptions form the ingredients for self-talk, self-understanding, self-confidence, or, sadly, self-loathing. Think carefully about the story you tell to others and thereby to yourself. For in your story lies the possible, the positive, the wisdom for your life—the WOWsdom!

CYNTHIA BIOTEAU, PH.D.

Dr. Cynthia Bioteau is the fifth president and first female CEO of Florida State College at Jacksonville, one of the state's largest institutions of higher education. Dr. Bioteau is widely recognized as a national leader in advocacy for public higher education and believes deeply that access to high-quality postsecondary education is key to healthy, literate communities, which are critical for the progress of us all.

EXPLORE

the POSSIBLE

To believe in what is possible
is giving yourself
permission to live fully!

BE AN INDIVIDUAL IN A SOCIETY THAT SHUNS DIFFERENCE

IMANI HOPE

Imani has learned a great deal about herself and other young people throughout her career in public education, teaching in the Philadelphia school system and now in New York City. Raised in Miami and Orlando, her studies and work experience have taken her across the country in pursuit of improving education outcomes in urban areas. A passionate believer in creating positive networks, experiencing life to its fullest, and commitment to self, Imani embodies a life of the positive and the possible.

Dear Me at Fifteen,

Hello from twenty years in the future! A lot has changed in the world; let me tell you. Teenagers now have Snapchat and Instagram, Twitter and the Kardashians (don't even ask). But one thing remains the same, and that is the struggle of finding yourself as a young person. Right now you are in a transition period in life. You are, like many of your friends and peers, struggling to find your own identity and to be an individual in an environment that shuns difference.

Explore the Possible

TRY OUT FOR THE PLAY!

TRY NEW FOODS!

Add your own:

_____
_____
_____

COMFORT ZONE

Add your own:

_____
_____
_____

TRAVEL!

HOLA! LEARN A NEW LANGUAGE!

Here are a few key things to remember as you continue on your journey of self-realization and growth:

1) You will be judged by the company you keep.

It may sound self-serving, but strive to surround yourself with people who bring your life richness and depth and for whom you can do the same. **Your friends are a reflection of you and you of them;** make sure you like what you're seeing in the mirror.

2) Don't judge yourself based on what others think, judge yourself on what you know.

The world will judge based on factors you can't change; **it will judge you on your gender and your race** and that is a reality of life. **Never** let those perceptions **cloud your self-worth or dim your light.** As Oprah once said, "What other people think of me is none of my business."

3) Take advantage of every opportunity you can to expand your WORLD view.

I know that **interning** over the summer or **volunteering** after track practice and on weekends doesn't sound awesome right now, but trust me: you will appreciate the chances you have to expand your perspective. Travel, try new foods, learn another language, try out for that play. Step outside of your comfort zone often and yours will be a life of continuous growth.

4) And lastly, BE YOURSELF!

I wish I could tell you that in the future you will live in a world that values women who are bold, opinionated, and daring, but that's not always the case. But you are all of these things and **what I can promise you is that being true to yourself will keep you grounded in self no matter what goes on around you.**

Love,
Imani (Thirty-Six)

Explore the Possible

LET'S GET COMFORTABLE WITH THE UNCOMFORTABLE

START!

You know, that thing, that opportunity you want to try, but it scares you and you don't think you have the skills or the confidence to do it. YOU DO and CAN! Take the first step; it could be your hardest, but it is the MOST important.

KEEP GOING

Once you get started, DON'T STOP! Momentum can make all the difference in whether or not you succeed.

PUSH THROUGH THE DOUBTS

Doubts are totally normal. If you give into them, though, it will be harder to succeed. You know that little voice that squeaks in your head? Don't listen! Instead, provide positive self-talk. In the end, you will look back and be amazed at what you have accomplished and overcome.

GIVE YOURSELF A PAT ON THE BACK

Taking that moment to celebrate you is so important. DO IT, FEEL IT, COMMIT TO IT! It is exactly this feeling you will use to motivate you again and again!

DO IT ALL AGAIN

Stepping out of your comfort zone gets easier with practice. You have done it once, now do it again!

A LETTER TO
LITTLE A

ANNIKA SORENSTAM

Annika is the greatest female golfer of our generation and is often regarded as the best of all time. During her fifteen year, Hall of Fame career, she rewrote the LPGA and Ladies European Tour record books, won countless awards, and changed the way women's golf was played, viewed, and covered. An entrepreneur and industry leader, Annika is taking all of the lessons she learned along the way and teaching them to her daughter, Ava. Her letter below is excerpted from a longer version available at annikasorenstam.com.

Dear Ava,

Rather than tell myself all the things I wish I had known or lessons I've picked up, I'm writing to you, my Little A. I did not feel "love at first sight" with golf. When I was a little girl, I'd rather be skiing, playing other sports, or spending time with family. Just like you. In case you do end up following Mama's footsteps, in life or in golf, here's some of what I know so far. (And to the young girls reading who want to be athletes, hopefully you learn something, too.)

Keep painting and playing the piano. Keep swimming. Keep playing basketball and t-ball and riding horses, which we know how much you love. Golf will always be there, if you want it. Just be ready for whatever you want to do. Just like you, I wasn't so keen to get a club in my hands and thought golf was too slow and boring. I loved all other sports—soccer, tennis, skiing—which kept me busy for nine and a half months of the year. But for the two or so months of summer holidays, Auntie Charlotta and I would be on the golf course. But here's the thing: my sister and I rarely actually golfed. We'd sit on your Grandma and Grandpa's pull-carts and pretend we were riding ponies as they'd pull us along the fairway. We'd pick up golf balls on the range to earn a little bit of money—those were the days before the range cart that you try to hit with shots scooped them up. We'd play soccer on the driving range with our friends.

We'd walk to a lake on the outside of the course, not far from the 14th hole, and then we'd jump in because it was hot. Then we'd walk back to the course when it was time for lunch or get an ice cream at the clubhouse. Literally, anything but golf. As a matter of fact, we weren't members of the club where my parents played, so when we did finally practice our putting, the general manager would come out and yell at my sister and me. We'd run away, and when we thought he was gone, we would sneak out and putt unaccompanied again. (Mama's allowed to putt now, even though I'm still not a member.) So that was my introduction to golf. I pretended to ride ponies, hung out with my sister, and just had fun. But I didn't hit any shots.

And having fun is all I want you to do right now, Ava. Just keep playing and exploring and trying new things. I really didn't start going to training camps until I was twelve, which some parents today think is really late for starting any sport. Nowadays many of the best young girl golfers probably break par when they're twelve. (I'll teach you what that means, eventually.) But you know what happened when I turned twelve? I was a little more ready for golf. **And it wasn't until I was sixteen that I said I'm ready to really focus on this** and put all of the other sports on hold.

So Mama and Daddy will keep taking you to t-ball or any other activity until you tell us no more. Because if I had only specialized in my first love of tennis when I was your age, I never would've tried golf. And as good as I know you are at golf now, if you stop when you're seventeen or eighteen because you've lost the desire or burnt out, what's the point? Many kids get pushed for the wrong reasons. Grandma and Grandpa never pushed and were always very supportive. **For me, it all came from the heart.** I wanted to do it. So, Ava, Daddy and I aren't going to push you either. So keep dressing up like a princess and take the time to explore what you love. Take all the time you need. Because one day you'll be a teenager and one thing that will be less of a debate is college.

College for me was sort of pure luck. I was representing Stockholm University in a tournament in Japan and playing with a young girl from the University of Arizona. Her coach came up to me and said, "Hey, would you like to come play for us?" Ava, let me tell you two things—

First: Saying YES was one of the BEST things I could Have ever done.

not just for my career but also for growing into a young woman. Second: Nothing can prepare you for Arizona in August. It's hotter than Orlando!

Grandma waved goodbye to me at the Stockholm airport and assured me that **the twenty-hour flight to Tucson was the same in both directions if I ever wanted to come home.** And for those first couple of months, it crossed my mind a few times. It was just me, my two suitcases, and my golf bag when I first arrived. That's it. Plus, it wasn't even guaranteed that I'd make the golf team. You fly all that way and then have to play eighteen holes to qualify. Thankfully, I made the team and I soon got settled in. But those first two or three months were tough. I'd studied chemical engineering back in Sweden, and while I kept taking those courses at Arizona, I was also taking English 101 just so I could learn the language better.

So whether in the U.S. or overseas, **go to college, Ava.** You'll grow up. It will end up being the most fun you will ever have. On your own, but with no real grown-up responsibilities. You'll see the world from another point of view. It may not seem like it now when you're six years old, but the world is small in a way, and you have so much to see. In the meantime, **find your passions, be ready for them, work hard for them, and appreciate them.**

FIND YOUR PASSIONS, Be Ready for them, work hard for them, AND APPRECIATE THEM.

And when the time comes, learn how to share your passion with others and inspire the next generation.

But promise me, my little sweetheart, to **enjoy the journey and wherever life takes you.** Take time to smell the roses along the way. If there is one thing I would have done throughout all my success on the course, it would have been that. There is a fine line between looking ahead to your next challenge and enjoying your most recent victory. I know you will learn that balance and I look forward to being a part of your journey.

Love,
Mama

BE CURIOUS

JULIE MORTON, Ph.D.

As President of Conscious Legacy Coaching, based in Toronto, Ontario, Julie's mission is to help people live the life they want so that they will leave the legacy they choose. Asking the big question—WHY?—leads you down a path of curiosity, one that has led Julie from teenager to Ph.D.

Dear Younger Me,

Life feels complicated. And truly, I am making life way harder for myself then I have to. The super easy secret to a really happy life (and something that took me years and years and years to learn) is that there are only two words I have to remember to be both happy and successful.

BE CURIOUS. (Curiosity means a genuine desire to notice, learn, and be drawn to things we find interesting.)

Two words for a happier life...that seems way too easy, right? There are three reasons why simply being curious significantly improved my life:

Curiosity makes life much more interesting:

- I am never bored (or boring) because there is always something to keep me interested.
- I am more likely to explore my world and feel comfortable taking risks, even if the unknown makes me a little nervous.
- Curious people are more likely to notice the beauty and wonder in the world around us, to search for meaning and purpose, and to find greater life satisfaction.

Being curious means that I will be more able to deal with life's challenges:

- It is really hard to be negative (anxious or overwhelmed) with things when I am curious about them.
- It is easier to learn and remember things in school that I find interesting.
- Curiosity is related to the same reward mechanisms in my brain (dopamine) that are involved in other experiences of pleasure like love, hunger, or sex. (Therefore my brain actually makes me happier when I am curious.)

When I am curious, I will develop better and longer lasting relationships:

- I meet and connect to a wider circle of people with whom I am open to forming deeper connections.
- I am a much better listener.
- I am more empathetic towards my friends and understanding about their circumstance.

A more interesting, happier life with good friends all starts with WHY? Thank you for learning to ask why.

Love,
Julie

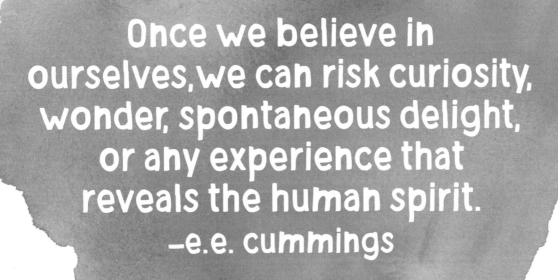

Once we believe in ourselves, we can risk curiosity, wonder, spontaneous delight, or any experience that reveals the human spirit.
—e.e. cummings

BOOST YOUR SPIRITS!

- Take a shower, trim your nails, wash your hair, or do whatever perks YOU up.
- DRESS UP or down, put on something that makes you feel special.
- Believe it or not, when you clean up the space around you, it really does help you feel better. You can make your bed and/or clean out your closets. A messy room can lead to messy thoughts and a mind which can become just as cluttered as your floor.
- Get rid of negative thoughts as negative self-talk keeps us from moving forward! The best remedy is to replace it with positive talk!
- Stand tall—with shoulders back, head up, and eyes forward, you will speak strength without opening your lips.
- Get active—taking even a short walk can really boost your outlook on life and clear your head!
- Do the things you've been putting off, they can hang over our heads like gray clouds.
- Do something for someone else. Volunteering has proven to be one of the best ways to boost your spirits and feel positive!

OVERCOME LIFE'S BULLIES

JACQUELYN PARISEAU

Jacquelyn works hard on and off the basketball court. Having recently graduated from Worcester Academy in Worcester, MA, Jackie is excited to continue on to college. She's always enjoyed participating in community service, clubs, and sports—especially basketball. Jackie hopes her story helps others to learn how to truly love themselves.

Dear "Future Bullies,"

I'd like you to know that I'm doing well. That **your words have never stopped me from being me.** That your hurtful actions have pushed me to strive for success. And for that I want to thank you. And if I were to see my bullies again, this is what I would want to say. **I would want them to realize that their words couldn't hurt me. And I'm hoping for anyone who has been bullied or, unfortunately, will be bullied that you can feel the same way too.**

Have STRENGTH. Be YOURSELF. Be Confident. Be able to be lighthearted. Be the person who sits with someone who is sitting alone.

Be the person who sticks up for others. Be the person who can create change in someone's life. Be able to stand up for yourself.

These are all important qualities as you grow to become the best person you can be.

Life has definitely not been easy, but it could've been much worse. **My eighth and ninth grade year, I was bullied to the point that I had to transfer schools.** I lost a lot of confidence in myself. I thought I wasn't good enough. I can remember being so disappointed in myself for not being "perfect." **But I've come to learn that I am perfect just the way I am** and that their opinions do not matter. Looking back, I wish I could've had these thoughts for myself. I wish I could have stuck up for myself when they tried to tear me down. I wish I could've been happy to be "me."

I've always been someone to hold in my emotions. I don't like to show defeat. However, I'm here to tell you that you shouldn't be afraid to express how you feel. That sometimes it's OK to be light-hearted, and not everything is serious. I've come to learn that life is too short to overthink everything. **As I was going through the bullying, my mom was diagnosed with breast cancer. I didn't want to burden anyone with what was going on. I felt so alone. I didn't know who to talk to. Now I would tell my past self to tell someone and to not be afraid to show what I'm feeling with everything that is happening. To know that it's OK to be vulnerable.** To have strength when everything seems to be falling apart.

Through all of these bad times, I've become a stronger person. I've learned how to stick up for others, to express my emotions, and especially how to love myself. Each person is different, and that's what makes you special. **You have to embrace who you are and enjoy every second.** As I've grown from girl to woman, I have been able to develop not only physically but emotionally and mentally as well. While you go on this same journey to discover yourself, remember to enjoy it. Remember that others' opinions don't matter. Remember that you are the best "you" that will ever live. Remember that you are perfect just the way you are.

Love,
Jackie (17)

"Vulnerability is the birthplace of love, belonging, joy, courage, empathy, and creativity. It is the source of hope, empathy, accountability, and authenticity. If we want greater clarity in our purpose or deeper and more meaningful spiritual lives, vulnerability is the path."

—Brené Brown,
Daring Greatly: How the Courage to Be Vulnerable Transforms the Way We Live, Love, Parent, and Lead

Vulnerability (n)—the quality or state of being exposed to the possibility of being attacked or harmed, either physically or emotionally.

ON CHOICES

AMY RUTH

Amy Ruth is the Chief Human Resource Officer for a $14 billion, not-for-profit health solutions organization, Guidewell Mutual Holdings, and leads the Senior HR Leadership Team with a passion for honesty, teamwork, happiness, and excellence. As we all are, Amy is the sum of her choices. Her choices led her to one of the top spots in the growing healthcare industry. Where will your choices lead you?

Think back to your youngest memory. How old were you? Chances are, you were probably about five or six years old. My earliest memory was when I was four: my mom died. As you probably can guess, I don't remember her at all because, like you, I don't have many memories from that age. I have a big family and I was her youngest child. **When I was younger, I used to think these facts defined who I was and that usually left me feeling lost.** Along the way, I realized that while these things certainly shaped who I am today, they do not define me. I am fifty years old now, and in my life, **I had to discover that life can be happy and sad, easy and hard. Life includes stuff that you may not like or ever understand.**

But I also learned that most of life involves choices.

We may not always have the ability to choose what happens to us, but we certainly have the power to choose how we respond. So today I try to live a life of positive choices.

Choose to love your family and friends. People may not stay in your life for as long as you would like them to, but they have been there for a reason and have touched your life along the way. Celebrate the good that comes from knowing and loving them.

Choose to be positive. You have a choice every day whether to let the "bad stuff" define who you are. I choose to focus on the positive and to be positive. Try it. I believe you can!

Choose good role models. I had wonderful people who encouraged and believed in me and taught me about believing in myself. Find the people in your life who believe in you and spend as much time with them as you can! They may be siblings, teachers, aunts, your parents, or a friend's parents. Realize what you admire about them and aim for that in your own life.

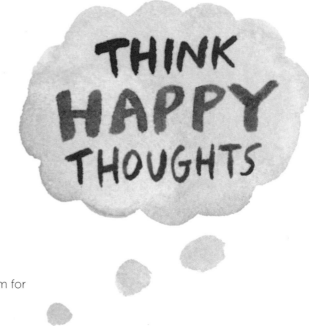

Choose how you will define success. For me, success has always been about making a difference in someone else's life. Find what makes you happy and pursue that. Success is not always about money and any really great opportunity should be about the way it allows you to grow and be happy.

Choose to be your best. Every day you get a choice as to how you are going to show up. Are you going to be happy or sad, try or give up, believe in yourself or fake it? You get to choose. Try choosing to be your best every day. You have great potential and you will be surprised how far this will take you. By being your best, you make those around you better, too.

Choose to be grateful. Be thankful for all you have and for those who have helped you. Help others in return. Learn to see yourself as others see you—your strengths and your weaknesses—and be grateful for the awareness. That is a key part to really allowing yourself to be your best.

Choose to have fun! If you are not having fun, you are cheating yourself—and you should never cheat yourself (or anyone else for that matter!). So, even if you don't like how things are starting out, you can choose to make it better in the end. Things today don't have to define your tomorrow. You choose.

The CHOICES are yours! XO Amy

IS THIS A GOOD CHOICE OR A BAD CHOICE?

1. Consider how your action will impact others.

2. Think of how the choice can either help or hurt you. Often a choice can do both—blurting out a hateful response to a friend in a moment of tension, for example. There is that moment of choice of how to best react.

3. When confused, take out a piece of paper and write a list of Pros (the good stuff) **and Cons** (the not-so-good stuff), the good and the bad. Taking the time to think through your options and see them on paper will help you understand and predict the positive and negative outcomes and consequences of your decisions.

First, identify a question or choice you need to make in your life. It can be about the classes you think you should take, friends to hang out with, colleges to apply to. Then list the why's—the Pros—and the why not's—the Cons—to get to the best choice.

MY BIG CHOICE: _____

_____

Think about a choice you need to make soon. Weigh the options, the Pros and Cons, below.

PRO:

1. _____

2. _____

3. _____

CON:

1. _____

2. _____

3. _____

"It is our choices that show what we truly are, far more than our abilities."
—JK Rowling

WHAT HAS BEEN YOUR HARDEST CHOICE SO FAR?

_____

_____

_____

_____

_____

_____

NO ONE IS PERFECT: DON'T JUDGE

THOMAS CARON

Tom is passionate about ensuring that students have the resources they need to be successful in school and in life and currently serves on the leadership team at City Year Jacksonville. City Year is a national organization of young adults who partner with teachers in the classroom to support the academic success of students in high-risk areas. Tom is married to his best friend, Alexa, and is the father of two daughters.

A note to all sons and daughters from a father, husband, brother, uncle, son, and a fellow human who has walked in shoes not all too different from yours at least once.

Start with, "All I need from you right now is for you to listen. I need to feel heard." These are magic words like abracadabra to get people to make time for you and open themselves to hear you. So write a note or pick up the phone and call someone. Start with, "All I need from you right now is for you to listen. I need to be heard," and everyone will recall when they were not heard and make time for you.

And then the really hard part: listen to the support they offer. If whoever you shared your story with sat there the whole time and listened, then clearly they care right?

Give them the respect they just showed you and actually listen to any help they offer. They probably have some life experience with your struggle—and if not, they can find someone who can relate to you.

When the day comes that you feel inadequate (at school, on the field, at a hobby, etc.) keep at it. Everyone at some point does not get it right on the first try. Sure, there are those around you who are quick learners or just get it right away. Great for them! Seriously, how cool for them. At some point there will be something that they, too, will not understand immediately, and you can be there to show them how to keep at it.

For when you realize your parents are not perfect: Yes, it's true. Your parents have and will make mistakes. They are experiencing life at the moment for the first time just as you are. I remember vividly the confusion and disappointment when I saw/learned of my parents' shortcomings. My advice to you: don't judge, don't expect perfection, and learn from their mistakes. "I will not be like that" and "I can do better" are powerful and have motivated each generation to improve. Someday soon you too will be the example for someone younger than you. Perhaps this is the circle of life and driver of change.

Take a breath. No one is perfect. It's OK to be wrong. The quickest way to fix it is to admit your fault, ask for forgiveness, and move on. If someone will not forgive you, that is unfortunate, but you should move on. If you forgive others, you too will be forgiven.

And for all days, especially when its not going right,

STOP AND BE GRATEFUL FOR WHAT IS IN YOUR FAVOR.

We all have those moments, days, weeks, or years when things go wrong or differently than we had hoped. However, something IS going right. Build the practice of listing all the things for which you are thankful. Start with the basics: you are alive—kudos to your cells, organs, bones, and body; your senses—I see, hear, taste—and keep listing until you get stuck—then push to find one more thing you are genuinely thankful for. Start this today and do it every day. It is the secret to happiness. Try it for a month—I dare you.

Imperfectly,
Tom

ACTIVE LISTENING

Active listening means we are:
present, pay attention, understand, respond,
and then remember what is being said.

Listening doesn't only happen with your ears. **You should use your eyes as well** to observe the other person's body language and how they act. Being an actively involved listener will allow you to learn more from the conversation than just listening to words alone.

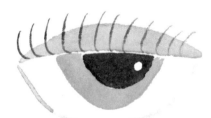 

TAKE your YOUR COMMUNICATION SKILLS TO THE NEXT LEVEL:

Put your personal feelings aside during the conversation, ask questions, and paraphrase, or repeat back, what you heard to the speaker to ensure understanding.

OPENING THE DOOR

SHAVONE STEELE

After some tough childhood circumstances, Shavone retreated inside her own head and stayed there for too long. Getting out of her shell in her 30's allowed her to embrace the outspokenness, confidence, and passion created through her experiences and personal history. With a daughter off to college and a new career on the horizon, she removed fear and said YES to more than she could have imagined.

Dear Ms. 13-Going-On-30,

Oh, Ms. Steele, always in a rush to grow up. Even as a child, you didn't want to sit at the kids' table—you stood in the kitchen with the women or in the yard with the men and had to prove you could hold your own with anyone—and you did! Though, in your rush to become a grown woman, you forgot a key to happiness: fun.

I know you just came through a few of your toughest years to date (trust me when I say "to date"), and you walked away so much more serious than you began. That seriousness will come in handy when you become a single mom at eighteen, move across the country without your daughter for six years, and return home to a dying grandmother and a mother you barely recognize. Girl, you know too well how to put your head down and get to work, be competent, and try to be one of the smartest people in the room.

What you don't know is that all this seriousness will close off your heart.

Explore the Possible

Popular wisdom says "You can never go home again." You proved that wrong. You came home from Chicago and blossomed—in no small part because you had a good therapist! As your prescription anti-anxiety meds kick in, an old friend will suggest you take classes down in St. Augustine for improv comedy. You do—and your first class will set you on a course you could never imagine. As you take these classes, you learn, through the tenets of improv, how to listen; how to be supportive; how to trust; how to take risks; and, finally, how to have fun. You are a master in class—always willing to step out first. Getting on stage, though, is a wholly different beast. Your anxiety, insecurity, and self-doubt show themselves each time in your bright red cheeks, flushed with the fear of failure. **The fear of failing or not being "enough" kept you from even trying for so many years.** That you even made it to the stage is an accomplishment. That you will eventually be part of a group who writes, produces, and performs two sold-out improv and sketch comedy shows seems unfathomable. **You will AMAZE yourself with what you can accomplish in a few short years and you will teach your daughter that, with enough gumption and trust in yourself,**

You Can Do ANYTHING

Since coming back home, you've done more than you could have imagined: performed for our troops in Guantanamo Bay, Cuba; gone camping and snorkeling; moved into a proper house; and laughed, a lot, with friends and strangers. Your heart may be less experienced than others at your age, and that's OK. At least you've learned to leave the door open.

All my love,
Shavone

FIVE STEPS TO BECOMING MENTALLY HEALTHY

To achieve balance in life, having some good friends, being social, and developing the tools to cope with the good struggles and difficult ones is a great starting place. Here are some tips from **Jamie Olken, LCSW** to guide you:

1. Social media. Are you attached to your phone? Take note: social media offers us connection and information that is crazy fast and helpful. Yet that same power can be addicting and sometimes make us numb to our feelings. Use social media for fun. If you feel like you are judging your self-worth by how many "likes" you get or you keep changing your posts because you feel insecure, then social media is not being used correctly. Don't forget digital communications are public and permanent!

2. Confidence. I was at a meeting with a well-known fashion designer, and she said woman are amazing, powerful, intelligent. And we ARE! Yet, so many of us are insecure. Think about this if you are feeling insecure: be nice to yourself and recognize what feels good about yourself. Don't let a negative thought or feeling linger. It's OK! Take the time to correct those negative thoughts and move forward. Remember—boys are insecure, too!

3. Listen to Your Body. If you don't feel well or think something is not right, ASK FOR HELP from friends, teachers, parents, family friends, or clergy. Don't wait until you feel really bad. Go ask now!

4. Be Open to People. Being vulnerable allows relationships to develop and deepen. If you are afraid of being hurt, know that everyone has that same fear. If you allow yourself to get to know someone and they get to know you, you could make a really great and unexpected friend.

5. Live, Laugh, and Try New Things. Get involved in different activities. Try new things while doing what already makes you feel good. If you love to sing—sing. If you love to play sports—join a team. If you want to try something new—try it and don't worry how good you are or what other people will say. The important part is to enjoy yourself.

Learn more about Jamie on page 55.

GENTLE REMINDERS

RYLANDER HANDFORD

Rylander just graduated from one of the nation's most prestigious public high schools, Stanton College Preparatory. Between a rigorous curriculum and a mom who serves as one of the highest ranking women in the U.S. Navy, Rylander, like many of us, is working hard on "figuring everything out."

Dear Future Me,

Hello, how are you? I wonder often what you are up to these days. I wonder if you still listen to Lorde or keep in touch with your brother. I wonder if you still like Halloween or stopped eating so much cookie dough like you said you would.

I wonder if you've figured everything out yet. Something my mom always told me, as I'm sure you'll remember, was to **not let the turkeys get you down.** As weird and bizarre as that phrase is, I hope you remember it. It's important to not let anything get you down. Don't lose confidence in yourself. You've got this.

Being in a military family was hard. Growing up, having to move every few years, brought a lot of sadness in saying goodbye to friends, childhood places, and houses, especially when you had just gotten used to calling them home. Moving, having to start all over, adapting, was hard. But it also brought a lot of good. You got to see and travel to so many places—Florida, Virginia, and Texas. You met so many different people, with different perspectives on life, and friends that you'll keep forever. **Moving taught you to be curious.** It taught you to constantly explore, improve, and change yourself. It made you who you are today.

Since I'm in high school, I see posters every day hanging in the classrooms that say the most cliché stuff, like "You Can Do It!" and "Hang in There!" Because you are out of high school now, you don't have that daily dose of inspiration in your life, which is why I am writing this letter.

You are strong and you are determined. Sometimes you just need reminding. Remember that time you had to give a speech on the junk food tax to the entire school and you were so scared? It turned out fine. Or when you had to go to a new high school and you were so nervous? It turned out OK, too! So, hang in there! And you CAN do this!

HANG IN THERE!

Remember that hard work pays off and life is unexpected and **everybody is human.** Remember your many homes and your victories and hard falls and how you worked your way to where you are now.

You know, you remind me of my younger self; after all, we have a lot in common. You and I, we both worked our butts off, and we have dreams that surpass the stars.

I've got a feeling you're going to make it. I believe in you.

See you soon,
Rylander Handford

Explore the Possible

START WITH A SMILE

KATIE HOLMAN

Katie is the new Supply Chain Director in India at General Mills and just left Minneapolis, MN, for the job of a lifetime. Katie's job is all about leading change, developing successful teams, and driving process improvements. She moved across the world with her husband, David, and daughters, Virginia and Louise. Her life has been underscored by change, and it's pretty likely yours will be, too.

Dear Thirteen-Year-Old Self,

I know you feel like the world is ending—Dad's just got a new assignment with the Air Force, so you're moving...again. You've finished seventh grade and you finally feel like you've found your place—your first year of middle school was awesome! You love your friends, love your teachers, and love your community! Life is good, so I know you're pretty mad at your parents for making you move. I promise that Mom is right when she tells you, **"Life's about changes, nothing ever stays the same."** And there's so much change...Change of house, change of school, change of town, change of people. What you don't know is that **change leads to growth, discovery, and new loves.**

On your first day, **smile when you see people.** It immediately opens up a connection and starts a conversation. In the future, this serves you so well. You understand firsthand what it's like to be the "new kid," so you go out of your way to be warm and approachable, welcoming new members of a team and making an effort to learn more about them and have them feel at home.

You'll become a connector—people want to be on your team, they reach out to you for advice, they have you lead difficult projects, because they know you care for people and can manage relationships. **And it all starts with a smile.**

Be brave and do something you've never done before—try out for the girls' basketball team. Sure, you've never played before, but you're so tall, what do you have to lose?! You may not get a lot of court time, but **you will learn that hard work and practice really does improve your skills! Most importantly, being on a team with a group of extraordinary girls teaches you that each girl has her own unique talent and when it's shared, you are unstoppable!** These girls are awesome—they make you laugh, challenge your thinking (You'll even start enjoying country music!), listen to you, and give you the confidence to go for the next thing, and the next thing beyond that. You're going to successfully face challenges through high school, college, and beyond because you practiced your skills and continued to surround yourself with extraordinary girls. **Seriously, you will not only survive but thrive in some pretty male-dominated areas (engineering, manufacturing) because of your girls.**

I know, you're still upset about moving and having to start all over, but you will grow so much from this. It sets you up to meet new and interesting people with a smile, to be brave and travel the world without fear, and to meet the most extraordinary group of girls from all walks of life.

Last thing, don't be too hard on Mom and Dad—they're trying their best, they love you, and they'll pick you up from basketball practice.

Sending you smiles,
Katie

HOW TO MAKE GOOD FIRST IMPRESSIONS

SMILE

SAY HELLO

STAND TALL

Ask a Question about them

Make EYE Contact

BE YOURSELF

When meeting new people
(in business, it's called "networking"):

- Don't be afraid to join in. Be yourself and know you are here for a good reason.

- Treat new people like they are already your friends—be honest, open, warm, and friendly.

- Ask questions and listen to what people are saying. Prepare questions in advance that will get others talking about themselves, such as, "What do you enjoy doing in your free time?"

- Show that you are engaged by making eye contact, smiling, and making them feel comfortable.

DEFINE YOURSELF BY YOUR STRENGTHS NOT YOUR WEAKNESSES

LISA SHALETT

Lisa is passionate about mentorship and committed to initiatives that emphasize leadership development, diversity, and innovation. Using her business background, most recently as the Global Head of Brand Marketing & Digital Strategy at Goldman Sachs, Lisa helps entrepreneurs and non-profit organizations succeed. Featured at the Fortune Most Powerful Women Summit, Lisa is a different kind of superhero.

Dear Young Lisa,

I know you love when people get right to the point, so I'll bring the wisdom. These are lessons that you will eventually learn, but I want you to have them NOW!

Be Your Own Source of Self-Confidence. If I asked you to name your weaknesses, I bet you could list them immediately. I remember what it was like to be a teenage girl—so many critics telling you your flaws and what you need to "fix", and harshest of all, the built-in critic inside your own head. These voices are Kryptonite! Train yourself to lower the volume of those voices, and avoid the self-doubt and insecurity they foster. Instead, **focus on your strengths.** If I asked you to name your strengths, could you tell me? Harder, right? So think about what you are really good at, be able to name those things, and find out if you are recognized by others for those things. Those skills and abilities you feel great about will be an important source of belief in yourself. (And over time you will discover more and more!) **Define yourself**

by those strengths, **not by your weaknesses.** Find confidence within—it will take you far, make you tough, and give you the courage to keep pushing yourself. It is the best superpower there is.

Recruit a Squad of Trusted Advisors. Make the effort to get to know teachers and grownups you respect and see others respect, and even people who are just a few years older than you. They are all potential mentors, role models, and advisors and could become invaluable sources of information and "safe spaces" to ask for help. Why would they want to help you? Because you are always full of positive energy and someone who tries her best, and spending time with you will inspire them and give them an opportunity to pay their successes forward. So don't tell me you're too shy, or convince yourself that you aren't important enough take up someone's time. If you start building relationships at this stage in your life, you will soon have a "Team Lisa" in your corner.

YOUR STRENGTHS ARE YOUR SUPERPOWERS

Name YOUR Top 3 Strengths:

1. _____

2. _____

3. _____

What would others see as your strengths?

1. _____

2. _____

3. _____

Defy Gravity. It is really easy and tempting to stay within your comfort zone—but it's when you step outside of it that you really learn. Your spending a summer in Japan at age fifteen, living with a Japanese family that spoke no English while you spoke no Japanese, becomes a major life experience for you, in ways you couldn't have imagined. You learn the importance of empathy and respect—for other perspectives and different ways of doing things. That experience goes on to affect your studies and interests, your career path, and your success as a leader. Keep experimenting, seeking smart risks, and changing it up even in small ways: eat your breakfast with chopsticks, or look at the same spot from different vantage points. Don't let gravity get in your way.

Put these in your utility belt, Wonder Woman!

With Love,
Your Older Self

1. Find what makes you unique and share it whole-heartedly with the world.

2. You'll need a couple of people who believe in you with all of their hearts—spend time with those people!

3. Muster all of the courage and fearlessness you can.

4.

BUILD YOUR BOARD

The best companies are led by a talented group of people who have talents in different areas called a board. You, too, can also have your own personal board. Your personal board should be full of people with a positive influence who provide honest, candid support, insights, and love. The people on your team are the ones you can call ANYTIME and know they will pick up.

Below is a board room table with five open chairs. On each chair, write down a person you want on your team and one reason they should be invited to sit at your table. Over time, the people in these chairs may change—and that's OK. Revisit your board room often and make sure the people at your table are guiding you in the right way.

PICK YOUR BOARD MEMBERS

influence (n)—the capacity to have an effect on the character, development, or behavior of someone or something, or the effect itself.

ALWAYS REMEMBER
WE ARE RESILIENT

LIEUTENANT LAKESHA BURTON

Lt. Burton is an inspiration to so many, serving as the Executive Director of the Jacksonville Police Athletic League. Kesha is only the second African American woman to earn the rank of Lieutenant in the 190-year history of Jacksonville law enforcement. Even though she had to take a tough road to her success, she earned it, to our collective betterment.

Dear Younger Kesha,

Let me begin by saying how much I love and appreciate you. Believe it or not, because of you, I am me! I think of you and your journey all the time because they were and continue to be great life lessons for me today as a woman. Flashbacks of you always leave me in awe!

I remember you being like any other normal child, energetic, inquisitive, sometimes mischievous, and wanting love and validation like any other 11-year-old. You loved to read books and watch documentaries about Jessie Owens because you wanted to one day run track in the Olympics.

Dark times began when your step-dad stole your dreams, your innocence, and childhood. **I know the abuse wasn't your fault** and your responses and reactions were normal for someone who had been sexually abused by an adult you trusted. On top of that, your mom chose him over you.

Explore the Possible

The anger, sadness, hurt, pain, low self-esteem, loneliness, brokenness, and hatred were all factors in why you were promiscuous, had a baby at fifteen, fought, drank alcohol, used drugs, engaged in unlawful activities, hurt others, became homeless, and were suicidal. WOW! How much can a person endure, especially a teenager?

You hit rock bottom and contemplated suicide, but you didn't do it. You were invited to attend a church revival—you are so glad you did.

After years of healing, you ultimately became the first African American homecoming queen and prom queen and later you were voted President of the Student Government by the school's student body.

GONE WERE THE years OF FEELING UGLY and NOT SMART

The highlight was receiving the Duval County "Turn Around" student award and winning that 1989 Pontiac car. You literally went from walking everywhere with your three-year-old son to driving your own car.

You were named female student athlete of the year, awarded a full scholarship to play college basketball, moved into your own apartment with your son, and graduated from college with a 4.0 GPA. This helped to catapult you into the next chapter of your life, where you took over.

Always remember we are resilient, and Romans 8:37: "I am more than a conqueror!"

Love always,
Lakesha

POSITIVE THINKING and SELF TALK make a difference

Look in the mirror EVERY day and repeat these 3 things:

1) I AM WORTHY!
2) I CAN DO IT!
3) I WILL SUCCEED!

SAFETY MATTERS

STACY PENDARVIS, MSW, MA

Stacy is the Program Director for the Monique Burr Foundation for Children, Inc. A social worker and educator with two Master's degrees from East Carolina University, and twenty years experience in the child welfare and prevention field, Stacy has educated thousands of adults and children on various child protection issues and has managed multiple community and agency projects related to child protection.

Being a teenager in today's society brings with it challenges and safety concerns your parents never faced. One out of five girls just like you will experience bullying, cyberbullying, digital dangers, sexual assault, or human trafficking, and you can't think, "It won't happen to me."

I'm sure your parents set rules and guidelines to help keep you safe. But as you get older, become more independent, and take on more responsibility, you need to learn how to keep yourself safe. Here are Five Safety Rules from the **MBF Teen Safety Matters** program you can use to help you be successful and stay safe in any situation.

Safety Rule #1: Know What's Up

Knowing What's Up means you are aware of situations in your environment, and people around you, that may not be safe, both online and offline. It also means knowing things like staying with a friend at all times and memorizing your parents' and safe adults' cell phone numbers in case you lose your phone. When you are aware, you are empowered and less likely to be victimized.

Safety Rule #2: Spot RED Flags

Spotting Red Flags means using your awareness of safe versus unsafe situations to determine if someone's behavior or a social interaction, online or offline, is unsafe or inappropriate. Spotting Red Flags like bullying, cyberbullying, inappropriate online behavior, adults trying to trick, force, or manipulate teens into unsafe or inappropriate situations, and controlling behaviors or emotional or physical abuse between partners in a relationship will empower you to use the other Safety Rules to help you stay safe.

Safety Rule #3: Make a Move

Making a Move involves using good decision-making skills to respond to new or unsafe situations, both online or offline. You can Make a Move by getting away from unsafe situations or people or staying away from people and situations you recognize as unsafe. It also means helping a friend out of an unsafe situation, whether they recognize it's unsafe or not.

Safety Rule #4: Talk it Up

Talk it Up means knowing you have a voice and knowing you can use your voice if you or others are in an unsafe situation, online or offline. You can Talk It Up by saying "no" to someone violating your personal boundaries or demonstrating unsafe or inappropriate behaviors to you or others. Talking It Up also means telling a safe adult about unsafe or inappropriate situations or behaviors. Not reporting to avoid being seen as a "snitch" allows problems to continue to grow and may cause more damaging, long-term consequences to you or another teen.

Safety Rule #5: No Blame, No Shame

As you mature, you will encounter new people and situations and will make decisions about your own behavior. No matter what happens, it is important to know you should never feel ashamed to seek help and talk to a safe adult if you are unsafe or have been hurt. You are not to blame and it is never too late to tell. It's also important to know that if you have made an unsafe or inappropriate decision, talking to a Safe Adult can help you learn and stay safe.

You can learn more about staying safe at www.mbfteensafetymatters.org

The Monique Burr Foundation for Children is a nonprofit organization started by Edward Burr in 1997 on the one-year anniversary of the death of Monique Burr (1960–1996), his late wife, to continue her legacy of child protection and child advocacy. The Foundation's mission is to make a positive impact on the community at large, to create change in a family's life for the better, and to give hope in the life of a child by providing bullying and child abuse prevention safety education that is relevant to issues facing children today. I am proud to have been a friend of Monique and to serve to further this really important work focusing on keeping us safe!

MONIQUE BURR
FOUNDATION FOR CHILDREN

Explore the Possible

Embrace DIFFERENT

JAMIE OLKEN, LCSW

Jamie is an esteemed authority on the areas of women's health. She is a psychotherapist in New York City who specializes in treating adolescents with issues ranging from eating disorders, to bullying, to substance abuse.

Dear JB,

All of your hard work, self reflection, and "being different" made you a wonderful adult. When you struggled with thinking differently than the "group" and when you voiced your opinion that was different than the "group," you didn't know it was going to be thought of as you being a leader.

> **When you felt sad, ugly, fat, and alone, one day you would realize that YOU were not being nice to yourself.**

You could have asked for help, though it took time for you to understand that you didn't have to feel badly and alone. Your friends did care and they were feeling the same awkwardness that you were.

School was important. You were with really smart kids. You didn't have to be first in your class to be a successful adult. **Having a well-rounded academic and social education was the right thing to strive for.**

WOWsdom! The Girl's Guide to the Positive and the Possible

55

You didn't have to be a bully. You didn't have to make others feel like you did when you felt weird or awkward. The bad feelings would change as the years went on. Your parents guessed a lot of the time. They really didn't know for sure what to do. They used a lot of common sense and good luck. The only thing they knew for sure was the importance of family and friends. They knew that you didn't have to have to the same values as your friends and that it was important to respect all values, even if they were different than yours.

Don't be afraid of difference—different looking, different acting, different religions, or different languages. Ask people what they think and listen. Truly listen. Differences should not make you feel afraid; step into that space—learn and grow.

Your Core Values Remain and only got STRONGER and CLEARER as you got older.

You weren't going to marry Joe so you didn't have to worry about breaking up with him. You could have done it earlier and had many more high school experiences. It has taken time and you learned to listen to the voice that tells you to move on.

You were always a good person and loved life. It was that good attitude that surrounded you with amazing friends and trust. Continue to trust yourself and embrace the differences that make the world such an interesting place. It will help you to develop the skills and become the core of the person you will be.

With love,
Jamie

TRAILBLAZERS

"No one changes the world who isn't obsessed."
–Billie Jean King, Women's Tennis Champion, Visionary, Pioneer, and Legend

"Courage, sacrifice, determination, commitment, toughness, heart, talent, guts. That's what little girls are made of; the heck with sugar and spice."
–Bethany Hamilton, Surfer and Author

"The success of every woman should be the inspiration to another. We should raise each other up. Make sure you're very courageous: be strong, be extremely kind, and above all be humble."
–Serena Williams, a top ten women's tennis player since 1999, and the player with the most Grand Slam titles in tennis (women OR men)

"Dribble til you can't see anymore, then turn on the lights."
–Diana Taurasi, WNBA Champion with Phoenix Mercury and four-time Olympic Gold Medalist, USA Basketball

"I'm scared of failure all the time, but I'm not scared enough to stop trying."
–Ronda Rousey, former UFC Women's Bantamweight Champion

"Dedication, determination, and desire is what it takes."
–Jackie Joyner-Kersee, four-time U.S. Women's Track and Field Olympian, including three gold medals

EMBRACE

THE POSITIVE

Seeing the glass as half full gives you the best head start in filling it all the way!

SAY IT OUT LOUD TO THE UNIVERSE

TINA LIFFORD

Tina currently stars as Aunt Vi in the highly acclaimed television series Queen Sugar *on OWN–from executive producers Oprah Winfrey and award-winning filmmaker Ava DuVernay. She is also known for her role as the CIA Director on* Scandal *and the mother-in-law on NBC's* Parenthood. *Tina is also the founder of* The Inner Fitness Project. *Through straight-talk workshops, Tina teaches women to thrive by accessing their innate creativity, resilience, and strength. Learn more at www.tinalifford.com.*

Dear Young Tina,

First, let me say I am so very excited that you were born. Without you, I could not have grown into who I am. Your hopes became my life, your challenges the lessons I needed to strengthen and prepare me for life. Thank you. You've taught me patience, made me resilient, and, through you, I have learned to trust myself and have faith.

So in your future moments of doubt, or when you fear you have made a horrible mistake, remember me shining brightly inside of you, already happy and successful. Don't worry about me or our future. Be optimistic instead. Focus on what you want and who you want to become and I will show up. **Having optimism and hope and maintaining a healthy focus on your dreams and goals will always help you forge ahead.**

Embrace the Positive

Speaking of mistakes...Along the way you will make what feels like mistakes. Here's a big secret: **Mistakes are never mistakes when we embrace them and learn from them.** Then they become fodder for a successful long-term outcome. During rough times or calm, be compassionate and kind to yourself always. Adopt the perspective that first and foremost you are innately worthy and divinely conceived. Therefore, **there is never—ever—a justifiable reason for you to speak poorly of yourself or to treat yourself harshly in any way**—not for any reason, at anytime, under any circumstances. This is simply unacceptable.

Such vigilant self-loving care is the best gift you can give to us. It helps me develop the kind of real and reliable confidence that allows me to walk into any room and feel comfortable and worthy. Adopting a steadfast sense of your innate worth also allows me to have resilience—the ability to get up and try again and again as I pursue any dream or endeavor. It encourages me to challenge my limits and reach beyond them. This will be most helpful in those times when some old hurt or problem seems too big for me to conquer. **With a strong sense of worth and resilience, we can dare to adopt the belief that we were not made to endlessly suffer, but to thrive.** With this in mind, we can look at our circumstances and dare to believe there must be a way through them to the other side. **Remember the saying, "If you believe a thing is possible, then it is."**

WHAT DO YOU BELIEVE IS POSSIBLE?

1. _____

2. _____

3. _____

More importantly, however, developing a self-loving perspective makes us act like Teflon in the face of abusive, ignorant, or mean-spirited people. Their actions and words will not stick and weigh us down. No matter their words or actions, when you remind yourself that you are innately worthy and divinely conceived, you maintain a healthy hold on yourself and win in spite of their actions.

Here are a few key things to remember:

Meditate. Meditation will teach you to know what's real and important. It will help you learn to challenge your thoughts and to ignore the thoughts that are harmful or left over from past experience.

When your heart yearns to be an actress (or for anything else), listen to it. Many people will tell you that your dreams are not possible. Daddy will tell you that actors don't make money and that most of them are unhappy. Pay other people's comments about your dreams no mind. Again, **when you sense in your heart that something is possible, know that it is.** And know that **realizing your dreams takes work.** Stay committed to your dreams, and grow yourself in the ways that your dreams require for stability.

Never give up! Find the opportunity in the failure, and search for freedom from your fears. Your brain is powerful. With better information and tools, you can change anything about your life that distresses you.

Release all people and things from the responsibility of making you happy. The boys you will pine over are just boys. They are not your happiness. Learn to be happy no matter what and understand that relationships come second and that they take a lot of work. The best people to have in your life are the ones that see you, appreciate you, enjoy you, and want the best for you.

You are precious and unique. I am your champion. You are my hope. I am your expansion and growth. Because of you and the choices you make, I get to experience our life as an amazing journey. Thank you. Be strong, have fun, and work to be happy.

I love you.
Tina

Embrace the Positive

Tina Lifford's LOVE THYSELF

1. Mistakes are never mistakes when we embrace them and learn from them.

2. There is never—ever—a justifiable reason for you to speak poorly of yourself or to treat yourself harshly in any way.

3. Developing a self-loving perspective makes us act like Teflon in the face of abusive, ignorant, or mean-spirited people. Their actions and words will not stick and weigh us down.

OFFICE WORK

BY LAURA HOFFMAN

I was a senior in high school
when a dog-tired fireman
at a cafeteria career fair
told me
maybe you should try office work
instead

I forgot his glazed eyes
and the pink
that set, stinging
into my cheeks

until the day
that I
and my platoon of sisters
marched defiantly
on the cold, cracked asphalt
of Parris Island
held out our earth-stained palms
and became United States Marines

no one told us then

that maybe WE

should try office work

instead

The women that I served with are now and will always be my sisters. We are truly "the fewer the prouder," and no one can ever take that away from us.

Laura Hoffman

LAURA HOFFMAN

Laura is a United States Marine Corps veteran currently pursuing her undergraduate degree in English and a proud mom. Hoffman's most recent work appears in: Bop Dead City, Twisted Sister Lit Mag, Clear Poetry, Pouch, and The Bangalore Review.

SHOULDERING
THE PAIN AND THE GAIN

DR. LUCY SHAFFER CROFT

Dr. Croft, Associate Vice President for Student Affairs at the University of North Florida, knows about leadership. She emphasizes a wellness approach to effective leadership, incorporating the whole mind and body into leadership, and she enjoys inspiring students, writing for professional journals, volunteering for non-profit organizations, and participating in marathons and triathlons. She has come to realize that what set her apart is now what gives her strength and a deeper purpose.

To My Twelve-Year-Old Self,

Let me give you a little warning. And a lot of hope.

Like your older brothers and sister, you're a gifted athlete. Living up to your family's reputation for being scholar-athletes comes pretty easily, and I know you love everything about it right now. Yes, you're struggling to find confidence in reading and writing, but you find your groove on the athletic fields, in the pool, and on the track.

Your natural coordination and competitive drive is a gift. **Maybe you're a little bit of a tomboy but so what?** How fun is it to be the first one—boy or girl—to climb the rope, run 600 yards, do more pull-ups and push-ups. In your heart, you know this is who you were born to be and I know how much you love winning.

Now for that warning: all the time you spend doing these things you love, especially the hours in the pool, means you'll soon start standing out in a different way too. As you grow physically, you'll become stronger than most of your peers and those tan shoulders will broaden—just enough to stand out a little.

You will soon consider your shoulders your nemesis; you'll get teased and you'll endure some awful name-calling too horrible to recite. **You will soon develop an unhealthy body image that will haunt you for years**—decades, actually. It breaks my heart to let you know things will turn ugly and all the fun you're having right now isn't going to last. I'm sorry.

But here's what I've learned, and here's what you need to know. None of that matters. None of it. **It may take decades for the weight to literally lift off those shoulders: that weight that says you're not good enough, fast enough, or smart enough.** The weight of conformity and impossible norms. The days will eventually pass when you care what people think. This part is so important; just know it is **those who find fault with others that have issues within themselves.**

You will make peace with the fact that you have broad shoulders. Beautiful broad shoulders that embrace the past and stand strong for those who come after you. They represent who you are and what you love and that part of yourself that stands apart and above others. They are not a fault; they are a hard-earned treasure.

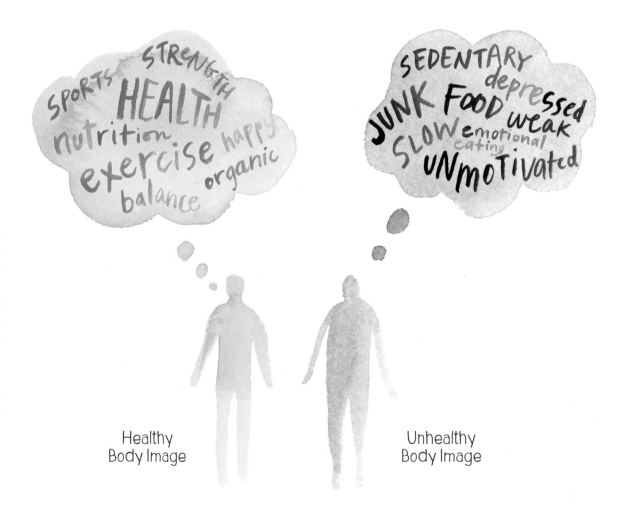

Healthy
Body Image

Unhealthy
Body Image

Embrace the Positive

I ask not for a lighter burden, but for broader shoulders.
—Proverb

Don't hide behind your special abilities: celebrate yourself and provide space for others to do the same. Your shoulders represent your intrinsic power and the strength of those who came before so you can, in turn, provide the strength for others to follow. They let you lift others up to be their unique selves—celebrating every facet of what makes them special. **Everyone needs shoulders to stand upon and that's what you're here for.**

You are an individual. Everyone is an individual. We aren't meant to be someone else and life's rewards don't come from conformity but from staying true to yourself—the rewards are beyond imagination.

Years from now, that joy you feel in the pool, on the track, and on the field will return and with it will also come wisdom. You know that joy now and you will know that joy again when you're older—and those years between are the time when **you need to stand on your own shoulders and celebrate you.**

In strength,
Lucy

FOCUS on FITNESS

Get into the mindset of taking care of your body. The benefits will serve you well throughout your life! Incorporate these health & fitness tips into your daily routine and experience the power of exercise and its positive affect on your physical, mental, and social well-being!

1. Drink a glass of water first thing when you wake up. Try to drink up to six 12-oz bottles of water a day—one at every meal and three more throughout the day.

2. Put on some music and every time the chorus of the song is on, do squats, squat jumps (jump up as you come up from a squat), and lunges (long steps, dipping your knee toward the ground). Do 10 of each exercise during the chorus. Two to three upbeat songs will do the trick!

3. Stand in the middle of your door and reach for the top of the frame, then bend and reach for your toes. When you stretch, it should feel good as your spine (backbone) expands and muscles loosen.

4. Watching tv, you can still be active. During commercials, do a plank (rest your body on your elbows and toes) and count to 20, then do 15 sit-ups, 10 pelvic lifts (lie on your back with bent knees and raise your pelvis), and 5 push-ups!

5. Let the palm of your hand help you with portions. If it doesn't fit in the palm of your hand, it's too much. And don't skip meals!

Fitness should be a part of your daily life. When it is, you help preserve the MOST IMPORTANT thing in your life—**your health!**

SHANAN HOY

Shanan grew up in California where she received her degree in Exercise Science, Kinesiology at CSU Sacramento. Shanan has actively pursued being an Aerobic, Kickboxing, and Strength Training instructor, a two-time Ms. Fitness Competitor, and Group and Personal Trainer in her sixteen years in fitness. As a mother to two children, she continues to pursue her passion of health and fitness as a personal trainer and is now the owner of Focus Fitness, a gym that inspires people to be healthy every day.

Embrace the Positive

SPEAK your TRUTH especially with YOURSELF

RASHEIKA FULTON

At fifteen, and from the Generation WOW stage in 2014, Rasheika reminded us all that honesty is really the best policy—for others and, more importantly, for ourselves. Self-deception will keep you from success and happiness and writing your story can help you make sense of the toughest times. Now eighteen, she is off to college and continues practicing the honesty that has gotten her this far.

Dear Future Self,

I see you happier than you will ever know. Your smile ever-so-bright and your laugh so goofy that it becomes a beautiful part of nature.

You, my dear, have experienced many changes. I am forever grateful you made it through. You set your mind on what you want, and you show the ability to conquer things no matter how stressful they are.

There is so much that you faced and need to remember as you move into your future. Be grateful for growing up in the military service. The benefits are really good and have helped out a lot. You had a chance to live in different places. You know how to relocate, readjust, and move forward. You learned to be open-minded. You have a love for traveling—keep shooting for Madagascar!

You see that no one can teach you how to be an adult. You have to figure out what you can do and what you can't do. You MUST experience the process—**it's not easy, but it's quite doable!**

Friendships are important. Keeping them in check is the real skill. I can see how NOT getting stuck on hanging on to some current friendships is not the best way to go. Friendships come and go. I can see how being open to all sorts of people and relationships is beneficial because you never know how people will impact your life.

You Are not alone in THiS WORLD.

You can hear what others think and feel, but only you can make the best choices for yourself—especially for your physical and mental health.

Yes, you had the heartbreak experience—it happened. I get that it is about really understanding what you want at the time. I'm trusting I'll find that one person who is on the same path...

I want you to remember this: **when things get crazy and hard to figure out, write about it in your journal.** Be as detailed as you can and don't ever lie to yourself in your journal. Always speak your truth. Remember how CLEAR you get every time you do this. The next step after awareness is to take action. What makes you successful is your ability to take action, and this will make a difference in your life.

You inspire me to continue to strive for the success that I know will become of me.

Keep keeping it real, Osha!

With love,
Rasheika

IT'S NOT YOU IT'S THEM

SHIRA KITAY

It is never as easy as it looks. A three sport athlete, an outstanding student at a top prep school, Shira found the challenges she would face in high school would become the strengths she would rely on at the University of Michigan.

Dear Fourteen-Year-Old self,

Be yourself. I know starting at a new high school is hard, especially where the majority of kids have known each other since the first grade, but you are a smart, funny girl, and you should know that your peers will eventually see that.

Keep your head up. **It is a horrible feeling when girls tell you that you can't sit with them at lunch, that there's no room at the table for you.** As you walk away, probably to go eat in the library (even though you know that's against the rules), and you see them pull up a chair for someone else, stay confident—it's not you, it's them. It kind of sucks having to covertly eat your lunch in the library, but hey, at least you never have homework when you get home!

Fast forward two years...you're going to get to know one of those girls better in your AP U.S. History class, and you're going to get invited to her surprise birthday party, where you're going to ride in a limo and eat dinner at Ruth's Chris! And remember to be yourself, because everyone's going to laugh at your jokes all night.

Fast forward one more year...those same girls stop you in the parking lot before you get into your car, after you all enjoyed a delicious dinner together at Stonewood, and apologize for what they said to you freshman year, for being superficial and closed-minded. Obviously, you accept their apology, 'cause you're smart and **holding grudges is pointless.** (I told you people would eventually come to their senses!!)

Fast forward two more years. You're home from college for Thanksgiving, or should I say "Friendsgiving," surrounded by those same girls, enjoying a potluck before you all head back to school.

You're so good at that. I'm so proud of you for always going to your teachers' office hours and for trying three different sports. Joining Track & Field might even be one of your greatest decisions—walking onto the track, knowing no one else on the team, can be daunting, and you're going to make so many friends from it! **It's not easy to step out of your comfort zone, but you have absolutely nothing to lose. In fact, you'll have so much practice from high school, that it'll be easy for you in college** and will allow you to seize so many incredible opportunities.

Although you feel lonely right now, you should think about all the amazing friends and family that support you no matter what. Go home and call your camp friends: they will always have your back.

You have four years ahead of you, and I'll be honest, it doesn't go by quickly, so you have to make the most of it. Take challenging classes, create positive relationships with your teachers, become a club president, and most importantly, stay true to yourself!

You're doing great, trust me.
—Shira

Embrace the Positive

WITH A LOT OF HELP FROM MY FRIENDS

AUDREY MORAN

Audrey is the archetype for civic engagement. A top prosecutor, former Chief of Staff to the Mayor of Jacksonville, a passionate leader for a major not-for-profit for the homeless, and now the Senior Vice President for Social Responsibility and Community Advocacy at Baptist Health, Audrey carried the support of her friends every step of the way. As the mother of four, Audrey has been a textbook example of a true servant leader.

Dear Audrey,

At sixteen years old, your friends are your whole world. But friendship can be hard. Friends sometimes let you down. They find other friends—or you do. They find boyfriends—or you do. You need to remember that **one of the keys to happiness is being able to forgive and forget**. And that no matter how busy life gets, making time for your girlfriends is very important.

You don't know it yet, but your friends are going to become even more important to you as you get older. It is your girlfriends who will help you through that first pregnancy, first newborn, first toddler, and first teenager. They will hold your hand as you send your child to college, and then to a job in a distant city. **They will celebrate your successes and stand beside you when you fall**. Your husband is there—but not in the way your girlfriends are. **They get it.**

So, take care of your friendships. Because in doing so, you take care of you.

Your friend,
Audrey

A THIRTEEN YEAR OLD'S GUIDE TO BEING A GOOD FRIEND

You've heard it 1,000 times: **treat others the way you want to be treated.** It is SUPER important when it comes to being a good friend. Your friends should feel like they are in a safe spot when they are with you. Neither they, nor you, should feel uncomfortable around each other. So treat each other with the utmost respect, and kindness.

If you have a BFF, they want to be able to trust you with all their secrets, feelings, or anything else they may want to share with you. **Remember, your friend is trusting you to keep that information private, and it is really nasty if you went and told someone else.** They trusted YOU for a reason. Even though you may be great friends with someone, know that everyone has a "personal space bubble" and things they choose to keep to themselves. If you ask someone about something, and they tell you they want to keep it to themselves without sharing, respect that. Everyone has their "stuff" that they keep to themselves. So, don't push someone to tell you EVERYTHING because it will make them more distant from you as time goes on.

Learn to go with the flow. To be honest, this is where I struggle the most. Going with the flow means not always calling the shots. If your friends feel like they have no say in what you both are doing, they will drift away or be more distant. This tip doesn't just apply to friendship but to family as well. If the majority, or even just your parents, say they really want to do something, or that the family is going to someplace that you don't want to go to, just let it go. You will get your chance to do what you want; just let it go because it will make your family or friend happy, and as a friend or family member, you should want them to be happy.

LIZZY BULER

Lizzy is a lover of dance and music and art. Just hearing a random song will get her moving as she pursues her passion in dance and spending time with her friends. She lives in NYC, is a big sister to two brothers, and always looks on the bright side of things.

Embrace the Positive

Last but not least, be ok with change. If someone who you think is your BFF becomes friends with someone you don't like, or someone that is not the nicest to you, that's ok! Remember, if this friend is someone you rely on, they will always be there. Don't think that if they are friends with the "mean girl" they will automatically become mean, too. If they possess all of the traits I have shared with you, **you won't have anything to worry about.**

Write three things you love about YOUR best friend:

1. _____

2. _____

3. _____

Now, call them and tell them what you think!

CREATING POSITIVE FRIENDSHIPS

Friends should be a positive and supporting part of your life–if that is not the case, move on!

Friendships grow over time, like a flower. Water and feed it and the beautiful blooms will be yours to share.

Be open to creating new friendships and meeting new people.

Social media can be a positive way to build your own friend group. It can also destroy it, so be respectful and thoughtful and do not gossip. What goes around comes around.

The company you keep is so important. As Donna's grandmother always said, "if you lay down with the dogs, you wake up with fleas."

Be a good listener–share and be there!

CONFIDENCE IS ALL ABOUT FAKING IT UNTIL YOU MAKE IT.

THE BEST YOU!

LISA PALMER

Listening to the advice of others, particularly our families, isn't always easy. With the support and encouragement of her family, Lisa pursued an excellent education, earning an MBA at the prestigious Wharton School at the University of Pennsylvania. With an illustrious career, including as CFO and President of a public corporate real estate company, she also serves on the boards of several companies and has learned much from her friends and family, including her dad, John Palmer (see pg. 106).

Dear Fifteen-Year-Old Lisa:

I know things don't always seem so easy and fun these days. You worry that you aren't as pretty or attractive as the other girls in your tenth grade class. You worry that you aren't as cool as the popular kids. Because of that, you often struggle with doing certain things only because you think it will make you more popular or make others think better of you. Stop doing that. **Don't do something just because you think it will make others think better of you. Do the things that make you feel better about yourself.**

All you want is for these years to go by fast so you can go on to whatever is next, because that has to be better, right? Just last week you were hanging clothes on the clothesline with Mom and she said, "Don't wish for these years to go by faster, because when you're my age, you'll wish the years will go slower. Enjoy these years!" You don't know it now, but when you are her age, you will realize she's right.

In fact, it's amazing, but mom is almost always right.

In fact, it's amazing, but Mom is almost always right.

She was even right about not wanting you to hang out with those kids that hung out late at night on the street corner. It wasn't because it was a conspiracy to be sure you were never cool and popular... it was because, believe it or not, **Mom really does want what is best for you and has a lot more experience in that category.** It's hard to understand that now because there are times you really don't want to have anything to do with her. But don't push her too far away because when you are her age, she will be the best friend you've ever had. In fact, try to tell her you love her at least every now and then...she'll never forget that.

There are so many things that are SPECIAL and GREAT about you. YOU aren't like the other kids but that's OK— because YOU are YOU!

You have so many talents that will take you far. Stop putting pressure on yourself to be better, different. I'm not saying to stop working hard in school and in sports. **I'm just telling you to be the best YOU that you can be. When you work hard and do the best you can, good things will happen.** And they will happen beyond what you ever imagined. Keep studying. Keep practicing your sports. But most of all, keep laughing, keep having fun, and keep your real friends close. It is those things that will bring a smile to your face when you look back later in life on your high school years.

Enjoy!!
Lisa

Embrace the Positive

OUR FAMILIES ARE SMARTER THAN WE GIVE THEM CREDIT FOR

"Listen to Dad when he advised you to get your teacher's certificate in college."–Cindy Edelman

"My mom always said, 'if you don't ask, you don't get.' She's so right." –Donna Orender

"Say thank you to your parents as often as you can (I know, its hard to fight the eye-roll, but try). Their sacrifices make your life possible, and if you become half the parents they are you will be a huge success."–Akila Raman-Vaseghi

"You will miss them so much when they are gone. Enjoy the fun of siblings in the house before they leave. And, realize your parents are trying their best."–Allison Keller

"In fact, it is amazing, Mom is almost always right."–Lisa Palmer

"Your parents have and will make mistakes."–Tom Caron

THE COOL KIDS

Here's some advice to help you reconsider "cool."

"Being cool is being your own self, not doing something that someone else is telling you to do." –Vanessa Hudgens, actress

"The lion does not turn around when a small dog barks." –Proverb

"A flower does not think of competing with the flower next to it. It just blooms." –Proverb

TURN FEAR INTO JOY

LARA LOMBARDO

Lara is one special young woman. At seventeen, she was a published illustrator for several children's books and easily could have chosen illustration as her path. Lara had the dream to become a baker. Now the Head Pastry Chef at Seagull Bakery, Lara is redefining just what is possible for those with autism.

Dear Little Lara,

I wish I had known when I was growing up many things that I know now.

When I was younger, I used to worry a lot and was anxious about my future. I just wanted to be a baker because I loved desserts and watching professional baking shows. But I worried about things like working and taking baking lessons. But I really wish I'd learned baking skills at a younger age—say about twelve—instead of waiting until about eighteen. And if I'd had a chance to work at a restaurant or a bakery when I was sixteen or so, instead of twenty-one, then I wouldn't have been so worried all the time! And it would have been nice to meet people who liked to bake, too.

Embrace the Positive

I was also very anxious about my education when I was growing up. Especially, I worried a whole lot about writing papers and stories for English class. I remember I had to write about news events, taking telephone messages, proofreading, and editing. It was really hard for me to think about and I got really stressed out. Now I know I could just ask my teacher or a friend for help. I could've explained that I was nervous and I hated writing. **I know now that people need to ask for help when they're anxious or stressed. It's so much better than holding it in or getting angry later because of something else.**

And guess what, now I love to write! I write journals about my thoughts and feelings, and I'm writing a book! **My book is about independent living skills for people with autism.** I write every day, so now I know how important it is to learn to write and wish I'd realized that when I was growing up. Writing is a great way to express myself, especially since I still get stressed and anxious. Also I'm a professional pastry chef, so I'm achieving my goals. It's hard to know when you're younger that your future will be great!

With joy,
Lara

Celebrating Differences

I love Lara, her spirit, her talent, and her mom Carol, who is the most amazing angel. Their very special relationship has taught me and so many others how love and commitment can bring out the best in people with Intellectual and Developmental Disabilities, known as IDDs.

IDDs impact over 200 million people worldwide, and they can impact anyone. While most common causes are genetics, problems during pregnancy or childbirth, and childhood illness, the cause of IDD is unknown in most cases. Some of the most common diagnoses are Autism and Down Syndrome.

People with IDDs are like everyone else—they have unique interests, values, and personalities. They cherish their family and friends and are more than capable of contributing to the community. So the next time you see someone in your neighborhood that may have an IDD, be inclusive. Treat them like you would any other friend or acquaintance, adding a little extra patience. We become a better, more thoughtful, and inclusive community when we reach out and connect.

A FEW TIPS:

Speak directly to people with IDDs, not to the other people with them.

It's OK to offer help, but don't push it. Using open-ended questions is great! Also, think about telling them, "If you ever need any help just let me know."

When discussing IDDs, people without them are referred to as "typical" rather than normal. Let's be honest—is anyone really normal?

"Special Olympics is not just about people with intellectual disabilities; it's about unleashing the spirit to uncover the best in ourselves."
—Tim Shriver, Chairman of the Special Olympics

"I was thirty-two when I started cooking; up until then, I just ate."
—Julia Child, American chef and author

Embrace the Positive

LARA'S CHOCOLATE CHUNK COOKIES

"These cookies are super delicious and make people really happy. I love these cookies!"

8 oz brown sugar

4 oz white sugar

8 oz unsalted softened butter

2 eggs

16 oz flour

1 tsp baking soda

1 tsp sea salt

12 oz semi-sweet chocolate chips

Place butter and both sugars in a mixer with the paddle attachment. Beat on medium speed until smooth and combined. Add eggs and beat until creamy. Add flour, baking soda, and salt. Mix until combined. Add chocolate chips and mix until incorporated. Scoop dough onto a cookie sheet and press down slightly. Chill for twenty minutes.

Bake in a preheated 325 degree oven for 12-15 minutes.

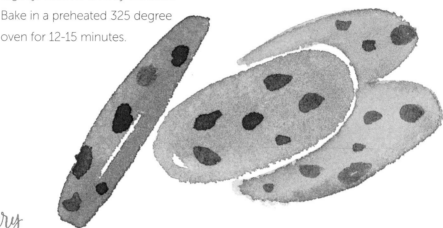

Seagull Bakery
CLASSIC & CONTEMPORARY DESSERTS

WHY COOK?

Self Sufficiency This means you can always take care of yourself and meet your own needs.

Save Money! Eating out even from a Dollar Menu is expensive. When you break down the cost of servings per meal, you will wind up saving a lot of money over time.

Create Better/Healthier Options Prepackaged and fast foods in particular have many additives that aren't great for us. You'll know exactly what you are eating if you cook with whole, fresh ingredients.

Learn to Express Yourself & Your Culture Our food comes from traditions, culturally and regionally. Keep those traditions alive and pass them on to your friends and family.

Appreciate Serving Others Providing nourishment for our loved ones is a gift we give and also receive. Knowing what we provide to others is sustaining will fill you with joy.

TO MY FUTURE MENTOR

JENNA LEVINE

As a teenager, we sometimes think we can do it all by ourselves. Jenna understands that having a person by your side as a coach, cheerleader, pusher, and mentor can make all the difference. She wrote a letter to her mentor—someone who helped her succeed during her last year at Stanton College Preparatory in Jacksonville, Florida, and then continued supporting her while at Syracuse University. With an interest in comedy and all things funny, Saturday Night Live *may be in her future!*

Dear Inspiration,

I appreciate your exceptional creativity and your ability to use this creativity to make history and set high standards for girls like me. I'm proud of my need to please others, even when it means sacrificing something of my own. **I feel overwhelmed with juggling everything I have going on, including making time for what makes me happy.**

I could use your help in realizing my own potential and in teaching me how to, most practically, play to my strengths. Because mentoring is a partnership between us, let me know if there is a way I can help you. For instance, I'm CPR certified, I make a mean grilled cheese, and I own an American Flag-patterned windbreaker that you could borrow for such patriotic events as baseball games, apple pie eating contests, and, my personal preference, for good luck on U.S. History tests.

Embrace the Positive

Can we arrange to meet in person or phone after I've overcome this inevitable awkward stage that all adolescent tween/teenagers must go through? Thank you. I appreciate how you do not even know I exist but you are here to help, motivate, and excite me.

~Peace and Blessings~
Jenna "J-Dawg" Levine

Hope has **no negativity.**
She has **no boundaries.**
Hope has a **better outlook**
For the future.
She doesn't judge others
For their downfalls.
When people stumble
And fall
She gives them
Courage and motivation
To move forward
And find peace.

—Incarcerated female juvenile
with Hope at Hand Inc.

Hope At Hand is a 501(c)3 nonprofit organization that provides art and poetry sessions to vulnerable and at-risk youth populations. Using creativity, language, art, and therapeutic approaches, they facilitate healing and personal growth for children and adolescents.

MAKING THE MOST OF MENTORSHIP

BY LISA SHALETT

Mentoring Is a Two-Way Street Don't expect the mentor to bring all the wisdom when there is a lot mentors can learn from mentees, too. If you're a mentee, think about what you can share with your mentor, and if you're a mentor, encourage your mentee to share their insights with you. Sharing strengthens relationships and makes them lasting and valuable.

Mentorship Provides a Safe Space Mentors offer a safe space to talk and a commitment to listen that can help a mentee navigate life choices, academic stresses, and family matters. They should give honest feedback, even if it's tough to hear.

Mentees Should Be Specific Help your mentor understand how you think they can help you— often mentors are listening for ways to be helpful; focus them and make it clear. Agree on these expectations and the rhythm of the relationship.

Cultivate a Group of Mentors Each mentor brings different perspectives, skills, and superpowers to the table. Have mentors both inside and outside of your existing network. Some male, some female. Think about the kinds of mentors you want and why. Mentors can be formal or informal.

Be Sensitive to a Mentor's Time Phone calls and Skype/Facetime can be great substitutes for in-person meetings once you know each other and when schedules get busy. Insisting on in-person meetings can mean that too much time goes by between conversations. Be thoughtful about when a mentor can help most, such as before/ after a major exam and education decisions.

Commitment Makes It Work Relationships, in general, work best when both parties want it to work and both are committed to making the time for and investment in the relationship. If that commitment isn't there, reconsider if this is the right relationship.

Attitude and Confidence Matter Mentees who come with a great attitude are energizing to be around and the kind of people that mentors want to align themselves with. Mentees who have even quiet confidence in themselves give their mentors the confidence they need to champion mentees and their needs.

Learn more about Lisa on page 46.

NOBODY'S PERFECT

SUSAN RYZEWIC, PH.D.

Susan is a dynamic and recognized leader and an analytical, intuitive, and compassionate problem solver who is respected in her family, her community, and in business and philanthropic communities. She leads the Remmer Family Foundation, creating a level playing field for girls through innovative programs in education, training, and support. Her journey led her down a road that could have ended much differently—her quest for perfection keeping success at bay.

Dear Younger Self,

My life would have been different if I had understood the lessons that I share below, and yet I would not be who I am.

I wish that I had focused more on my personal priorities and goals rather than on meeting my parents' expectations. My parents were examples of the American Dream—the first generation to go to college, both graduated from prestigious colleges on academic scholarships and both achieved financial success. They had high standards and expected their children to be excellent students, competitive athletes, and good-looking. I felt that I needed to be perfect to be loved.

NEWS FLASH: No one is loved for being perfect.

A quest for perfection contributes to setting and delivering on exceptionally high standards for performance. I encourage dedication and excellence, but **perfection is unattainable**. My striving toward this unattainable goal caused stress, contributed to emotional challenges, and created a debilitating fear of failure. My fear of failure resulted in chronic, last-minute, pre-deadline completion of projects and papers and a recurring sense of inadequacy.

Perfection was my enemy of completion and self-acceptance. When I was in sixth grade, I did not complete a music project that was due right after our February vacation. Rather than tell my parents and face the consequences, I feigned illness to stay home from school. That absence started a downward spiral that spanned decades. My shame led initially to psychosomatic, and eventually to real, illness. That deception then led to shame and future deceptions, with each subsequent deception further eroding my self-worth.

I was twenty-eight and writing my dissertation before I finally realized that I could change what I wrote and that finishing is better than perfect. I finally started writing and working through my paralysis. It makes me sad to realize all the time and energy that I wasted could have been used in more intentional, purposeful, and satisfying ways.

I was well into adulthood when I recognized that **mistakes are an essential part of growth and learning.** At twenty-five, I asked my husband if he ever made mistakes at work—and I was serious!

MY FEAR OF "BEING WRONG" INTERFERED with my ability to make Decisions OR TO BOLDLY Express my views.

My lack of confidence held me back in both my academic and professional advancement...and contributed to a significant financial loss.

It took time to identify that the lessons I learned, and how I changed, helped me to build my self-confidence, make decisions, take bold action, and learn from the past and focus on today to enhance the future.

Oh, younger Sue—the learning came late, and it was hard-won. Be sure to focus on today so your tomorrows will be better...and I can tell you they will be.

With love,
Susan

Embrace the Positive

ACCORDING TO PLAN

Few things ever go as planned. What is something that has not worked out for you? What did you learn from that moment?

_____

_____

_____

_____

Failing Gracefully

1. Don't make it personal. Personalizing failure can wreak havoc on our self-esteem and confidence.

2. Look at the failure without emotions, suspending feelings of anger, frustration, blame, or regret. Why did you fail? What might have produced a better outcome? Was the failure completely beyond your control? After gathering the facts, step back and ask yourself, "What did I learn from this?" Think about how you will apply this newfound insight going forward.

3. Stop dwelling on it. Obsessing over failure does not change the outcome. In fact, it will only intensify the outcome, trapping you in an emotional doom-loop that disables you from moving on.

4. Release the need for approval of others. Often our fear of failure is rooted in our fear of being judged and losing others' respect and esteem.

5. Flip the script. Shift from a negative perspective ("If I fail, it means I am stupid, weak, incapable, and am destined to fall short") and embrace the positive ("If I fail, I am one step closer to succeeding; I am smarter and more savvy because the knowledge I've gained through this experience").

LIVE, LAUGH, LOVE THROUGH IT ALL

PIPER CUSH

Piper is a rising Junior in Ponte Vedra, Florida. Her epic move from Connecticut to Florida taught her to open herself up to many different "friend groups." She is the co-founder of the Generation WOW club at Ponte Vedra High School, dreams of playing volleyball in college, and wants to make her impact on the world.

Dear My Future Self,

Right now you are living through some of the best years of your life. You have gone through so much just by one small move from Connecticut to Florida. You have lost your friends, your childhood home, your opportunities in the musical world, but you gained many memories.

Although eighth grade was a torturous year and you felt trapped, you have escaped and flourished throughout your first two years of high school. I hope that you continue to spread your wings and share your love, joy, and passion with others. I hope you branch out more and grow as a person and continue to make new friends. I also hope that you continue to challenge yourself at school and **surprise yourself every year:** it was just yesterday that you got an amazing score on an AP test.

Another thing I hope for is for you to have made an impact.

Embrace the Positive

Whether it's related to global warming or performing in a Broadway show, I will be proud. **I believe you can become a positive influence for many people far and wide.** I hope that you are well-traveled and have been exposed to many cultures, for this will help you understand your life in a new light.

You finally made your school's volleyball team. You have worked so hard for the past three years to achieve this goal. I hope it encourages you to keep pushing hard and to improve each and every day. Nothing is out of your reach, especially when you have monkey arms and can jump 9'7" (hopefully higher by now).

Thinking about it now, I hope you get into an amazing college that will help kick-start your life out of high school. It could be Georgetown, Duke, Johns Hopkins, or any other school, yet I will be proud no matter what you achieve. And I also hope that you have chosen a career path in Math. Even though you only began taking Algebra 2 Honors and Pre-Calculus Honors this year, **I believe you can make an impact with something that makes you smile every day.**

I also hope that by now you have learned to keep in contact with people better.

Before the move, you totally lied by saying you would text your friends every day. Fix that.

Speaking of friends, I hope that you continue to make some of the best decisions ever and stay with people that love you for you and make you smile every day!

Keep doing what you do best: live, love, and laugh.

Yours truly,
Piper Cush (2016)

MOUNTAINS OF SUCCESS

DAVID EMMANUEL

Though David studied history and pre-law at Wittenberg University in Ohio, he has been focused on global human resources for the past thirty years, currently sharing his talents and experience at APR Energy, a global energy provider. He is also the Principal at Root to Route, LLC., and the Director of the Florida Human Resources Executive Council. Even with such great roles, David believes his most important leadership role is as the father of his incredible daughter.

Dear Jordan,

Since your mother passed, I know that there are times when the dad in me is not as understanding as the mom you miss. The challenge of becoming both Daddy and Momma has been a hard one. However, there has never been a second in your life where my love for you, my daughter, has waned. Having you as my daughter continues to be the greatest blessing. I write this letter to you because I want you to know how proud I am of the woman you have become.

Some days, I sit solemnly thinking about all the people we have lost in the last several years: your mother, your paternal grandfather, your Aunt Alta, your maternal grandfather, and now your grandmother. It has not been easy on you and still you have kept your focus on realizing your career dreams as well as staying true to your core values, things that make all of us proud of you.

Embrace the Positive

Over the past 24 months, you have been working and living in NYC, something that so many dream about and that you are living. You deciding to follow your dreams and not travel the beaten path was not a choice that I was 100% sold on, and despite my opinions, you have persevered. Not only did you know what you were saying about leaving that Administrative Assistant position, you have proven that yours was the best course for you. Your choices have led to various critiques and criticism. Standing up to the critics and criticism has proven that you are strong enough to stand up for what you believe in. You have done this in an outstanding manner—THAT is what truly matters.

Jordan, you are a high achiever and you are uniquely capable and qualified to meet and exceed your wildest dreams. None of us are perfect, yet I believe you are perfectly suited to continue to climb your mountain of success. I pray that you will remain steadfast, confident, and vigilant in pursuit of your short and long-term career, personal and life goals. I will always be here standing beside you.

It is important to remember that, as you pursue your goals, achieving them is not always a straight line and on a prescribed timetable. You will have obstacles of all sorts, and with your ingenuity and tenacity, you will find a path to success that will be uniquely yours.

LASTLY, DON'T ever FORGeT THAT you Have People WHo LOVE and RESPECT you AND WHO WILL ALWays be willing to lend a hand, an ear, and a caring thouGHT

You are a fine young woman who brings honor to her family, friends, and anyone you meet.

I love you dearly,
Daddy

SOCIAL MEDIA
APPROACH WITH CAUTION

As someone who believes in the power of storytelling, I spend most of my days helping others—whether that be people or companies—becoming their own best storytellers. While there are numerous tips I share, the one at the top of the list is simple: **you be in charge of your own story!**

Life throws many things our way and although we can't control what happens to us or even how people respond to our words and actions, we can be responsible for what we post—and why we post it—on social media. **How do you do this? By simply asking yourself these four questions:**

1. Am I seeking approval?

Social media is designed to be addictive. BE AWARE! We post a picture of our cute dog and instantly ten people give us a "thumbs up" on Facebook or a "heart" on Instagram. The more positive comments we get, the happier we become. The effect is only temporary and when our mood begins to dip the minute the "likes" become less, we are setting ourselves up for a big emotional fall. **Did you know that eighth graders who are heavy users of social media increase their risk of depression by 27 percent?*** Be careful to not lose your sense of who you are in the approval of others.

New York Times columnist David Brooks recently said, "Social media promises an end to loneliness but actually produces an increase in solitude." **YIKES!**

Writer, social scientist, and self-proclaimed neuroscience enthusiast Mohadesa Najumi said: **"The woman who does not require validation from anyone is the most feared individual on the planet."** I believe that and I want you to believe that, too!

2. Am I feeling frustrated, sad, or angry?

This is a great rule for "real life" and social media—never respond from a place of frustration, sadness, or anger. Social media amplifies our feelings—negative or positive—and once we post our comments or image, we invite others into the conversation. Those posts, even if you eventually delete them, leave their mark on those who have read them. **What may seem "snarky" or "sassy" to you can be interpreted VERY differently by them.**

If someone has made you mad or hurt your feelings, put down the phone, close the laptop, or power off the tablet. Take a few moments to focus on things which make you grateful—the friend that drove you home from

*footnote to Atlantic article, Have Smartphones Destroyed a Generation?, Jeane M. Twenge, September 2017 issue

Embrace the Positive

school, the rain that stopped as soon as you realized you forgot your umbrella, the new playlist Spotify just "discovered" for you—anything at all! Think about things you are thankful for until those negative feelings subside.

3. Is this something I would say in person?

Standing behind a keyboard and screen makes us all very brave. We tend to forget that there are actual people—with actual feelings—on the other side of our technological worlds. Social media is about creating conversations—it's about dialogues, not monologues (hence the word "social")—and **respecting our online relationships in the same way we would our offline relationships will go a long way towards creating good in this world.**

If you are getting ready to post a comment that you would never say if the person stood before you, **don't post it!** Even if you strongly disagree with what someone has said, don't hash it out over social media. Instead, call them, invite them to sit down and have a face-to-face discussion. Can't imagine doing that? Then you shouldn't post the comment.

4. Is this a moment?

At lunch the other day a friend wouldn't let us dig into our sandwiches until she got the perfect shot for her Instagram page. And there was that time when our neighbor stopped my daughter in the driveway to tell her how sorry she was she didn't make the middle school soccer team, a fact she would never had known had I not blasted it out to my Facebook friends in a post.

Not every image needs to be snapped, not every moment needs to be shared. When we spend so much time trying to get the perfect shot or come up with the perfect hashtag, we miss out on one of the great joys of life—creating memories that are just between our closest friends and family members. Respect the moment and the people in it.

If you consider these four questions before you post anything on social media, you will control your own story. **You ensure that who you are and what you value shines through even before someone meets you.**

PATTI MINGLIN

With a degree in English and Communications, Patti graduated from Ball State University doing two things really well: writing and talking. Those two skills fed into Patti's passion for storytelling, helped her move up in the newspaper industry, and led her to launch her own content marketing company, Go Girl Communications. It's no surprise that Patti contributes regularly to publications and blogs including sharing her voice from the stage of as part of the Listen to Your Mother *Chicago cast in 2015. Patti resides outside of Chicago with her husband and three children.*

KEEPIN' IT REAL

YVETTE ANGELIQUE HYATER-ADAMS, MA-TLA

Yvette Angelique is a writer, teaching-artist, and narrative practitioner in applied behavioral science. She runs Narratives for Change and is a highly sought-after leadership coach and facilitator for writing workshops, developer of women's and girl's programs, social action writer, and cultural activist. When Yvette Angelique has something to say or share, you know she is going to bring honesty and the capital-t Truth to every conversation.

Dear Yvette Angel,

Imagination and creativity are your greatest gifts. **All that time daydreaming, reading, and fantasizing in your bedroom pays off.** Believe it or not, you don't end up as the famous girl-version of George Benson playing the guitar you trained so hard for. You lay down your Les Paul Custom for an elegant rollerball pen. Instead of scribbling chords on staff paper, you write poetry and prose that sing like music. You have to experience the power of writing and transformative change. Paul's murder and its rippling effect on the family finally rest in peace through writing. You find your voice. Now you help others who are silenced and traumatized free their voices through writing.

Remember how you were the first in junior high school to take wood shop, metal work, and leather class instead of the traditional cooking and sewing for girls? **Well, this pattern of being the first woman—and woman of color—stepping in a "for men only" domain continues.** Unapologetically, you move

Embrace the Positive

through many career lanes, bringing an artist's mindset and a woman's prowess as a Senior Vice President in banking, President and CEO of a consulting firm, and President of an international educational institution. You take strategic risks and make bold moves. All of your experiences and learnings come together—arts, business, leadership, and social change. Blending creative writing and narrative inquiry become a platform for your work in the world.

You did well with picking a great mate and end up with two fantastic children. Your family is close, jokes run amuck, and the love is thicker than dried mud.

By the way, you finally accept your curvaceous counterculture body, towering height, big feet, and twisty wild locs; **you love who you are.** It all fits your style these days—Bohemian Chic. It wasn't easy getting here. **You face situations where men try to strip you of your dignity and personal safety with unwanted touches, sexual harassment, and discrimination.** You show great resilience. Bottomline: your creative-artistic identity keeps you sane.

The summer vacations down the country, walking the land with Aunt Lucy, grow into making you an avid hiker. Climbing rocky paths in places like the Grand Canyon and vortexes in Sedona is your humble communion with the power of the Universe. Life experiences lead you to advocate for a socially-just and pluralistic society and a sense of belonging. Your Engaged Buddhist practice helps you on this path to freedom.

EVERY CHOICE IS THE RIGHT ONE- NEGATIVE or POSITIVE BECAUSE IT RESULTS IN PERSONAL GROWTH

Keep journaling, meditating, learning, and connecting; let your truth speak. Some will love how you do this, and others will not. Keeping it real is just how you like it. Stay the course.

Be Creative and Be Well,
Yvette Angelique

TAKE A

Take a breath! We've read so many incredible stories. I have to tell you, all of these women and teens fill me with admiration. Here is a chance for you to reflect. What stories stand out for you? Lessons? Words? What made you smile, reflect, perhaps tear up? Who do you want to know more about? By the way, you will be able to connect in a deeper way with many of these women on our website, **wowsdom.com**, and at this year's Generation WOW event.

I often like to talk about having strong shoulders, like Lucy Croft (page 65) did. We do stand on the shoulders of those who came before us—that's why we need to make sure ours are strong as we pay it forward for those who come after us.

WHO DO YOU ADMIRE?

Women you know personally:

_____

_____

Women you know about:

_____

_____

Embrace the Positive

BREATH

For me, an amazing woman that comes to mind is **Fran Kinney**—the first woman to serve as president of a university in the southeast United States. She's a visionary thinker and the most positive person. Her philosophy is simple: "I want people to move together and work together." **She's 100 years young and still counsels students and generously shares her wisdom.** Whom does she admire? MARGARET THATCHER, HER MOTHER, BERTHA BARTLETT, and MILITARY WIVES.

HER TOP 3 PIECES OF ADVICE:

Open your mind!

Life is not about "me," it is about "others."

Joy in learning comes from helping others. There are wonderful people everywhere: you just have to get to know them.

The challenges that women have faced are innumerable. By sticking together and supporting each other, we can create a culture of sharing. That's what this book is all about.

Ready to keep reading?

Onward!
Donna

FIND YOUR

PASSION

When you lose yourself in passionate pursuit, you will find yourself in love with life.

KNOW THYSELF

– Delphic Maxim

GERRY LAYBOURNE

Gerry is a serial entrepreneur who has had her finger on the pulse of the American media landscape for nearly forty years. With an impressive resume—including the first president of Nickelodeon and co-founding Oxygen Media with Oprah—Gerry's story seems like a fairy tale. In fact, it was the hard lessons she learned early on that helped keep her on a path to ever greater success and happiness.

Dear G (at nineteen),

Forget freshman year. OK, you didn't go to private school. OK, you had trouble learning how to read. **Stop counting the number of students who talk before you feel compelled to state your views in class. You have a different kind of brain.** Some kids think straight ahead; they learn from books and lectures. You have a lateral thinking brain that makes you very creative. You learn by doing, by listening hard, and by reading the room.

You butchered your freshman year because you did not know anything about drinking. You had never been to a bar. You felt out of place and you drank to feel you belonged.

You also do not memorize well and many first year courses require that. It never seemed important to you. You'd rather study people. And BTW in the distant future someone will invent the Internet and search engines and knowing facts and trivia will matter less. Just don't play Trivial Pursuit when that comes out. Stick with strategic games like Scrabble.

I am so proud of how you took stock in your sophomore year and realized you needed to get engaged and involved and outside of yourself. **You needed to do something for the greater good.** When you tried to run for your dorm presidency, your grade point average was too low so you had to petition Dean Drouilhet (aka The Warden) to let you run. **You told her that for you to be successful you needed responsibility and engagement and that the more you did the better you would do academically.** You promised her if she let you run, you'd get straight A's. She took the gamble. You got straight A's, you became the President of Davison House, you created an inclusive climate in your dorm, and you learned how to delegate.

What makes me proud is that you used self-knowledge to get you off a very bad track.

Dean Drouilhet will surprise you next year by putting you on the Master Planning Committee of Vassar College just as it decides to go co-ed. You will learn how to run a meeting, how to represent your constituency (students), how to gain consensus, how to build a plan, and imagine buildings.

All these things will matter as you go out into the world. And you graduated with honors.

With love fifty years later, G

Resilience

Resilience is a skill that has to be developed—like our muscles or learning a language. Resilience is what allows us to get knocked down and bounce back stronger than ever. Rather than letting failure overcome them and drain their resolve, resilient people find a way to rise from the ashes.

Develop your Resilience by:

KEEPING A POSITIVE ATTITUDE.

LOOKING ON THE BRIGHT OR OPTIMISTIC SIDE.

LEARNING TO KEEP YOUR EMOTIONS IN CHECK.

SEEING FAILURE AS A LESSON NOT A LIFE SENTENCE

FALL SEVEN TIMES AND STAND UP EIGHT.

- Japanese Proverb

THE POWER OF LEADING

Follow your passion. Your passion emerges when you realize what drives and ignites you—don't be afraid to follow it! When I was twenty one, the United Nations was organizing the largest-ever gathering of women leaders, and I was determined to go. So, I saved and borrowed and made my way to Beijing, China. The experience taught me the first lessons in leadership that ended up changing the trajectory of my life. I met women who had dedicated their lives to empowering others. I gained a sense of purpose that led me to an internship at the White House and then the State Department, where I joined the team that launched Vital Voices. To this day, my passion for women's leadership guides everything I do.

Mentorship leads to leadership. Mentors have been so integral to my leadership development. When a mentor shares experiences, knowledge, and power, they accelerate your growth as a leader. I believe a good mentor will celebrate your successes, and a great one will help you learn from your failures. It's important to realize that mentors don't take your hand and guide you forward, they're allies who stand behind you—win or lose. I know that I can't pay my mentors back, so I choose to pay it forward and mentor others. And that's the true power of mentorship—it fosters leadership and also sets off this incredible ripple effect of collective impact.

Failure isn't the opposite of success, it's a step closer to it. Failure ultimately leads you to success. In any journey, there's no avoiding failure. And as difficult and disappointing as it can be, it's also a chance to learn something. If you choose to be open to new lessons and have the courage to keep trying after you've failed at something, I can guarantee you'll go further than you ever expected.

ALYSE NELSON

Alyse is co-founder, president, and CEO of Vital Voices Global Partnership. Alyse has worked with woman leaders to develop training programs and international forums in over 140 countries and is the author of the best-selling book Vital Voices: The Power of Women Leading Change Around the World, *which shares the stories of remarkable, world-changing women. She provides the three lessons you need to lead.*

— OH THE — CHOICES YOU'LL MAKE

JOHN PALMER

Dads have a unique perspective on their children. Just ask John. John loves sports, traveling, great food, and exercising. He always seems to adopt his current hometown sports teams but can't shake his Philadelphia roots, so those teams are always closest to his heart! Even closer than the Phillies or the Eagles is his daughter, Lisa Palmer (see pg.77).

Dear Elle,

So far, so good, I'd say.

You're a beautiful, loving, kind, caring, considerate, playful, joyful, and smart young girl. You're on track to become a teenager who's got it together and then a fulfilled adult.

You already know that you are unique in the world, and you know that every living thing is unique. Although there are no guarantees in life, there are almost no limits other than your own abilities on what you can do or achieve.

I've watched and tried to help as you've become this kind, considerate, and caring girl and as you worried about every bug, every bird, every dog or cat, and every child who seems to be hurting or in danger and tried to help them out. I hope you'll never lose that compassion for others. It is beautiful

I've been here as you began to read and travel and learn so much about the world. I hope you'll continue to do that throughout your life. Dr. Seuss is right: "The more that you read, the more that you'll know, the more that you learn, the more places you'll go." And the more opportunities you'll find to be fulfilled–to find your passion.

you have the freedom to choose what you do with your EVERY DAY–no one can choose that for you.

And over the days and months and years, those choices you make every day will shape your life. You can choose a life of service to others, a life in which you try to make life better for other people, and maybe animals, which seems to be your passion now. Or you can choose to simply enjoy your own life, pursuing your intellectual, emotional, and spiritual interests. I hope that you can do both: continue to read and travel and study and learn and grow and become a learned and wise woman and also find a passion for a mission to help others.

I have just a few pieces of advice that I hope will help you on the way. Think about these as you go:

FAMILY and FRIENDS matter a lot.

I think it's hard to be happy alone in the world. Stay close to your family if you can, and as you gather friends, try to keep them. It can be a chore sometimes, but I am telling you, it's worth it. As you get older, you will realize more and more how fulfilling it can be to share your life with family and friends. Happiness blossoms when it is shared. And pain is eased when it is shared.

SPEAKING OF PAIN:

You will get hurt. When you share your life with others—animals and people—they will sometimes hurt you. It's part of life. Plow through.

DON'T FORCE YOURSELF TO make CHOICES TOO SOON.

If you're lucky, you will find a mission in life that fulfills you—makes you feel really good about yourself and your life. It might take some time and a few experiments before you find that mission; just keep trying things until you do.

TAKE CHARGE OF your own life.

It's the only thing that really belongs to you. Do not let other people make your big decisions!

The joy of life is pursuing your dreams. Dream big(!) and enjoy life.

I love you.
Dad

YOU DO NOT NEED PERMISSION TO BE UNSTOPPABLE

SIMONE EDWARDS

Simone, known as The Jamaican Hurricane, is a basketball player who played for the New York Liberty and the Seattle Storm and was the first Caribbean and first Jamaican player in the Women's National Basketball Association (WNBA). Her new book, Unstoppable (Diverse Writers Room), *published in 2017, offers a captivating portrait of Simone's relentless and passionate pursuit of a dream and her unwavering determination not to allow her circumstances to dictate her future.*

Dear Younger Me,

I am so proud of you. You have overcome your fear of being stuck in poverty and have held your head up high after being teased about your height and basketball abilities. **Growing up poor in a third-world country was no easy feat,** yet I was a happy child for most of my childhood. I tried relentlessly to be included in sports and games my older brothers played and I failed miserably. I was the youngest of four children and the only girl. This made me work even harder to be good at sports so they would include me. It took years. Then, finally, I was good enough for my brothers and, eventually, for the other boys in my village. Ultimately, I'd beat most of the guys in road races and never backed down no matter how rough they got with me when I played with them. They were not going to let a girl show them up and **I was not**

going to be excluded anymore because I was a girl. My bruises were reminders of my struggle to be accepted in a male-dominated sports world.

Too often, our lights and water went off in the village, which led to long walks with buckets to fetch water. We had a coal iron that was placed on hot coals or burning dry wood which was collected to make fire to cook and iron clothes. As early as six years old, my mother taught me to wash my clothes using a small wash-pan outside, make my bed, set the table, and clean the dishes and the house. My normal was hearing gunshots as they flew through the air, knowing death was present. However, despite the harsh realities of growing up in an impoverished, gang-infested village, hearing the sounds of gangsters running on top of our roof to escape from the police and the countless times police beat down our door in the wee hours of the morning, searching for gang men, I was still a happy child.

I believe growing up poor kept me humble.

It makes me appreciate the little things in life and taught me how to survive when I left my family to come to the USA for college at age seventeen. At one point in my life, I didn't know what I would do after high school. However, this didn't stop me from dreaming and setting goals that I thought deep down would only be imaginary goals. But I was given an educational opportunity I could not refuse and decided to work hard and stay focused so I could be successful. **Our lives can change at any second, so we should not give up on our dreams or bury our goals.** I am grateful that I got an opportunity to improve my life and in return I try to help improve the lives of others. **If anything, I learned that our present circumstances should not dictate our future.** You do not need permission to be unstoppable. You never gave up on basketball even as the hot pavement from the pestering sun burned your bare feet as you fought back tears knowing this was your way out of the ghetto in Kingston, Jamaica.

I know there were times when learning the game seemed difficult and complicated, but you were too determined to conquer it. I am glad you didn't give up even when your future was so blurred by your poverty.

your dreams of becoming successful kept you going, even if it seemed more like a fantasy.

Thanks for not listening to the people who teased you and called you names as you practiced basketball. Thanks for not complaining about your one pair of school and church shoes you kept taking to the shoemaker to fix because they were all you had.

Your struggles pushed you toward being a humble and tougher you. You will achieve things that were too far-fetched even in your dreams. Keep appreciating the little things and never give up, even when others tell you it's OK to. **Your success awaits you.** Keep trying to help those less fortunate because you will impact many whose lives you have touched. And you will even become the first Jamaican WNBA player.

Much love,
Simi

UNCERTAIN ANSWERS

DANIELLE BENNETT

Thirteen-year-old Danielle has so many questions for her future self—questions you probably do, too. As a rising freshman and middle child, just coming of age and moving around the country for her parents' work, Danielle is tackling some of the same feelings of uncertainty, fear, and insecurity that creep up on us all. Now settled in Washington, D.C., she continues to explore opportunities in the arts and to find her place in the world surrounded by friends, family, and a great sense of humor and courage.

Dear Big Me,

How are you? I hope you are well.

Currently, I am very lost with who I am. I danced my whole entire life. I recently decided to take a break from dance because I wasn't feeling the passion anymore. I have always been drawn to the arts, so are you doing something involved with the arts? Whatever you are doing, **I hope you enjoy it because you have a tendency of doing things for other people more than doing things for yourself.** I wonder if you still remember saying, "If I get into a dance company, I will be happy forever." Are you happy?

Are you close with your siblings? I hope you are because, as Mom always says, "You only have one brother and one sister." Right now, I can't seem to understand what is going on inside of their heads. Make sure to be happy for them and all of their successes. It has been very hard to do that now because it feels like

Jonah and Erika are always so much more successful than I am. My grades have always been lower, they seem to get along better with each other, and they seem to get along better with Mom and Dad. I feel like the odd woman out. Right now, I have been finding it hard to have faith in myself to be "successful," but

You need to have faith because there is always a light at the end of the tunnel.

How do you define success now? What's life like? What's the new technology? Mom thinks that I should take up something with technology or social media in the future. I love social media right now. Snapchat is currently the "big thing," but I know—in like four months—there is going to be some new social media coming out so I can't imagine what it's like for you currently. **Use social media wisely,** because, as mom ALWAYS says, "Although the latest and greatest creation might get you to believe that it disappears or that it is private...IT ISN'T!!! It may come back and haunt you forever."

I can't wait to find the answers to these questions in the future!

Love,
Little Me

"You have to accept whatever comes and the only important thing is that you meet it with courage and with the best that you have to give."
–Eleanor Roosevelt

FIND YOURSELF WHEN YOU ARE FEELING LOST

Think back to the last time you were having FUN—real "didn't pick up my phone, watch TV, or know where the time went" F-U-N. What were you doing? Do more of that! When you make a commitment to do more of the things that fully engross you and that you find to be truly fun, you may have found one of your passions.

Write about your hopes and dreams in your journal—and be honest. In your journal, feel free to think big as you explore your desires. As you reflect on what stirs in your heart, write down ways you can bring those hopes and dreams to life.

Lastly, make a mental note of the details in the world that catch your eye and make your heart flutter. In these details, often overlooked, we usually find themes and patterns that reveal our true needs, wants, and motivations. Listen, look, and reflect and watch your path unfold before your eyes.

TAMING THE BEAST OF ANXIETY

Learn to breathe. In through the nose, out through the mouth. The longer the better.

Get enough sleep. At least seven hours is the bare minimum.

Hang out with your friends and really laugh!

Play around and get silly!

Cut yourself some slack. You are doing better than you think!

Fight anxious thoughts in advance by preparing for the day ahead.

Visualize the positive.

Eat right. Small portions, colorful natural foods, lots of water.

Physical clutter equals mental clutter, so take time to clean up!

Find the time when you can completely disconnect and shut off all of your devices.

Express gratitude.

Find Your Passion

LEARN TO LISTEN AND
PRACTICE PATIENCE

ALLISON KELLER

Allison, as the Executive Vice President of Human Resources and Corporate Development at PGA TOUR and an attorney, is responsible for ensuring that the PGA TOUR recruits, retains, and motivates its highly-talented workforce. She is also responsible for motivating herself over the years and has learned a lot of lessons along the way that she shares with her daughters.

Dear Younger Self,

I first want to give you a hug and say, **"Everything is going to work out fine."** I know you worry about your future. Concern and worry about the future is OK to a point if it helps to motivate you, and I am here to tell you, take a deep breath and know, deep in your bones, all will be well!

The first thing I would like to tell you is that right now, **you have a sense that God is real**, and you crave a spiritual dimension in your life. I would tell you to run after God with all of your heart, soul, mind, and strength. His plans for you are bigger and better than anything you could imagine, and major decisions—such as who will I love? Will I marry? What career? Will I be a parent?—will carry a blessing and hope that is beyond the world's wisdom.

Learn to listen, really listen, to others. I mean this both from the perspective of hearing and understanding what is being told as well as empathy and learning to get behind the eyes of the person talking to you. Maybe read up on how to increase listening and comprehension because I assume in the future we will all be even more distracted with technology, so the discipline of listening is important. And the other side of listening—**understanding someone's heart**—will help you be a better friend and loved one. Sometimes people just need to be heard. Practice this.

Pay attention in Math and also take Finance courses. Finance is the language of business and the economy and I really can't think of any future profession, including parenting, where this isn't critical. **Understanding economics, finance, and basic accounting will be helpful in many areas.**

Practice patience. It is an unpopular virtue but is good for stress relief and for being a good person. You like to walk, talk, and move fast, but we shouldn't assume that the world will move at our speed. Practicing patience can help you to look around and see the beauty of the moment.

Don't be in such a hurry to get somewhere that you miss the now.

The cultural focus on looks and physical beauty is unrelenting—don't spend so much time on this. Young people, even with blemishes and braces, have such energy and vibrancy that it is so attractive. Trust me. Enjoy this time and don't try to change yourself. Dress your age and have fun with it! **Also, wear sunblock.**

Linger over that breakfast or visit with your grandparents. Try to mentally record their voice, their stories, their faces. You will miss them so much when they are gone. Enjoy the fun of siblings in the house before they leave. And realize **your parents are trying their best.** One day, you truly will enjoy their company and **realize they know more than it seems.**

Finally, sometimes you just have a bad day. It doesn't mean you have a bad life. You have a great life. Learn to call it a day, take a hot bath, and wake up fresh and get back at it.

All my love,
Your Older Self

MONEY DOES MATTER

Good financial habits are best begun as soon as possible. It's a good idea to learn what you can and ask your parents, caregivers, and teachers questions. It will make a huge difference in promoting positive financial behavior. Here are three of my favorite tips to help develop good money habits:

USE YOUR ALLOWANCE SPARINGLY

If you are lucky enough to have a weekly allowance (I didn't!), don't squander it. Figure out what you will spend, what you will save (10% is a good start), and what you will share with those who are less fortunate. Be sure to keep track of everything you spend!

LEARN THE BASICS OF INTEREST

With a savings account, a bank will pay you interest—a tiny bit of extra money earned on the amount deposited. This extra bit of interest can help you earn money with your money. To see how it works, check out the compound interest calculator at <u>investor.gov</u>. The flip-side of earning interest is when you have to pay interest on money that you borrow, like credit cards, mortgages, and student loans. Be sure to understand what your responsibilities are and use credit sparingly and only when really needed!

UNDERSTANDING TAXES

When you get that first job, learn the difference between gross pay (before taxes are taken out) and net pay (the amount you take home). This is a perfect opportunity to learn how the government taxes each worker's income, as well as an ideal time to start saving for retirement...the earlier you begin, the better!

JILL SCHLESINGER

Jill Schlesinger, CFP®, is the Emmy-nominated Business Analyst for CBS News. Jill appears on CBS radio and television stations nationwide covering the economy, markets, investing, and anything else with a dollar sign.

SAVE, SAVE, SAVE!

The importance and value of saving can't be overstated. There is a genuine confidence that comes with having a stash of cash in the bank you can access in lean times or to purchase a coveted item. The ability to delay gratification and give yourself a cushion will ensure you have less anxiety when you are paying bills, when something unexpected comes up, and when you are ready to retire. If you are in the habit early, saving as an adult when you finally land a good job won't be so hard.

CHECKING & SAVINGS ACCOUNT

Getting a checking account gives you a safe and secure place to deposit and withdraw your money and deposit checks. Checking accounts are available through an online bank, traditional bank, or credit union, with each having its advantages. You will need proof of identification, such as your Social Security card and state ID or driver's license, whether you open your account online or in person at the bank. When you use these accounts, be sure to track what you spend (checks and debit card purchases) and deposit (returns/credits and paychecks) so you don't spend more than your available balance (known as an overdraft). The fees for going over—Even by a dollar!—can be as high as $35. Imagine paying almost $40 for a latte because you didn't track your spending!

FINANCIAL SUCCESS STARTS NOW

1. **Start saving early**, even as little as five percent of your income, to help with future expenses—whether expected or unexpected.

2. **Make sure you have enough money to cover your necessary personal expenses**—identify needs versus wants and avoid impulse buying.

3. **Always shop around** for the best deal.

4. **Use credit wisely**—only take on credit card (or any) debt if you have a plan to pay it back. Interest charges can be expensive.

5. **Demonstrating your ability to responsibly manage your money** will help you borrow money in the future for large purchases, such as a car or house.

—Kelly B. Madden, Executive Vice President, Florida Division Manager, Wells Fargo

WRITING CHECKS

Though you may not write many checks because everything is moving to digital transactions, you will likely get a few over the course of your life and it's a good idea to know what it all means.

1. **Date** — the date the check is written
2. **Maker** — the account holder
3. **Payee** — person/business to whom the check is written
4. **Signature line** — signature of maker
5. **Written amount** — the amount in numbers
6. **Legal amount** — the amount written in words
7. **Check number** — printed on the check twice once at the top and again in the *MICR* line at the bottom of the check
8. **Banking information** — the name of the bank and the American Banking Association number
9. **Account and routing numbers** — appear on the bottom of the check in the *MICR* line

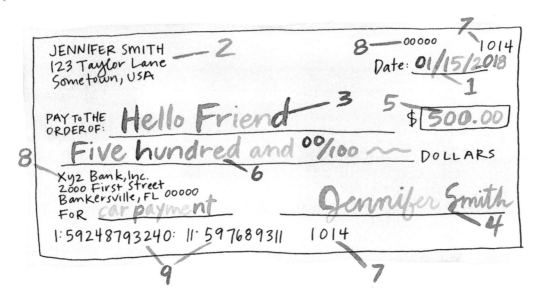

KEEPING YOUR MONEY SAFE

Popular money transfer services like PayPal or Venmo offer great ways to easily pay your friends instead of using cash or checks. Remember, like with any other digital accounts, to keep your password secure and safe! Do not share your personal identification number (PIN) with anyone, do not use financial apps on unsecure wi-fi (think coffee shops or airports), and use caution when clicking links in emails from unknown senders. It is better to NOT click on a link from an unknown sender.

YOU DESERVE IT

PRISCILLA MEJIA

Priscilla is another high school girl who WOWed us onstage at Generation WOW. Even at seventeen, and a junior at Darnell Cookman School of the Medical Arts in Jacksonville, FL, she had an exceptionally clear vision of her goals, who she wants to be when she grows up, and the values which drive her young life.

Dear future Priscilla,

I really hope that you reached your long-term goals because you deserve it! I know as a sixteen-year-old you would tell me that you would like to improve on your social, emotional, and physical development.

I expect that you married the man of your dreams and had a huge, beautiful wedding! I hope that you guys always enjoy each other and have fabulous times together, but, most importantly, **that you stand by each other's side through the difficult moments in life.**

Don't continue on a low level of social development by being quiet and worrying about what others say. Aspire to inspire. Become unique.

PUT yourself out there and talk to more people.

Find Your Passion

You will regret not growing socially. Stay close to Ally, Abby, Jay-Jay, and Deep—they are keepers! When you need to turn to someone, they will be there: through thick and thin, no matter what. They will become almost like blood family. They are truly the type of people you know you can't lose!

I hope you become the world's best pediatrician. Continue your education and go to college. There are so many that want you, but make sure you don't choose one too far because you are needed by your family. Don't forget your duties at church as head of the children's ministry.

Oh and missy! I know how much you love to eat sweets, but be careful! After you eat that yummy bread, pastry, or ice cream, go out and run with your hubby! Burn those calories because you don't want to be looking like Santa Claus at age thirty-two. Joining the gym will make the experience not only benefit your health but also your happiness. By doing your exercise together as a family, this will help **bind the family closer through all kinds of moments.**

Start and finish your goals, especially the ones about making a difference in the world. **When you die, all that will remain of you is your dust and your history.** So make sure you make your imprint on the Earth, so that when people in 10,000 years say your name, they associate it with positive things like caring, helpful, treated everyone equal, compassionate, and optimistic. Make sure you do EVERYTHING to the best of your abilities. Be that difference that we want!

Most importantly, enjoy the time you have, make the best of every situation, and smile!

Sincerely yours,
Priscilla Mejia

10 HEALTHY TIPS FOR YOU

By Kathryn Pearson Peyton, MD

GET ENOUGH SLEEP

Sleep affects everything, particularly your immune system and level of happiness. A rested mind improves efficiency and performance.

DRINK WATER

Yes, we "wilt" just like plants. You need to be peeing colorless or light yellow urine several times a day (dark yellow means you are not hydrated enough).

KNOW YOUR BODY

Take time to learn what is and looks normal. Take notes on what triggers headaches (getting enough fluids?) or rashes or belly pain or acne...Learn how your normal bumpy breast feels—easiest to evaluate after each menstrual cycle ("period") has ended. Know the normal appearance of your moles so that you may detect changes.

NEVER SMOKE

Not only does smoke affect your lungs and heart, it affects your skin. You don't want to look fifty years old when you are only thirty-five!

WALK QUICKLY

Movement is good for your heart and clearing the "air in your head."

EAT TO LIVE

The most important decision we make every day is what we put in our mouths. Period. Take notes on how you feel after eating certain foods: what gives you energy and what zaps your energy. Avoid eating to fill a sadness or void or anxiety (walk instead).

FLOSS

Everyone older than fifty wishes they had flossed more.

FLOSS

FIND FRIENDS WHO MAKE YOU BELLY LAUGH

Laughter produces good neurochemicals that improve your immune system and well-being.

TAKE Time to "JUST BE"

Mindfulness reduces anxiety, improves response to stressors, strengthens resilience, improves focus, reduces pain, and improves performance.

NURTURE RELATIONSHIPS WITH FAMILY & FRIENDS

Connections produce neurochemicals that improve longevity and well-being.

BE FRI ST END

PRESCRIPTION
(20 MINUTES EACH DAY)

1) Turn off technology   2) Get comfortable   3) Focus on your breath

4) Meditate your way: counting breaths to four or ten, yoga, tai chi, walking quietly in nature

5) As distractions / thoughts enter your mind, acknowledge them and then return your focus to your breathing

Learn more about Dr. Peyton on pg. 185

BECOMING A CATALYST

AMANDA MICKELSON

Amanda stands in the shadow of no one. Her independence, social engagement, and absolute sense of self inspires teens and adults who have the pleasure of knowing her. Deeply interested in Egyptology and women's issues, she is committed to changing the world and being the change—no questions asked.

Dear Amanda,

Hey, you. It's me. And by "me," I mean you, except with more acne and less life experience. I am seventeen, and it's my senior year in high school. **I'm still trying to figure out what it means to be me,** and I'm still figuring out what it means to be a strong woman. So I thought I might pick your brain—after all, you happen to be the only person who knows me better than I know myself.

How's life? Are you still in touch with the people who helped you? Did you ever get better at cooking? Did you end up studying Egyptology? Did you end up studying Gender and Sexuality? Did you end up playing a sport in college? Varsity? Club? Are you happy? Did you ever write that book? Do you still want to? Have you been to Egypt yet? Is it safe? Does it matter? Did you get into grad school? Who are your friends? What are they like? Are you still obsessed with peppermint tea? Are you still a word nerd? Is

Catalyst (n)—(1) a substance that increases the rate of a chemical reaction without itself undergoing any permanent chemical change. (2) A person or thing that precipitates an event.

the fact that "literal" has come to mean "figurative" still driving you nuts? Have you figured out how that happened yet? Do you still care? Of course, I have infinite questions for you, but you're probably curious about me, too.

At seventeen, you were excited for the future, at home in the past, and in love with the present. Kids called you "Grandma" because you took care of them, and it meant the world to you.

you did not allow your competitiveness to overshadow your mission to SUPPORT and RESPECT your peers.

You realized that you were not an academic; instead, you were a scholar, and with guidance from some brilliant women, you came to understand the difference. You were a quixotic dreamer surrounded by realists and logicians. Ludwig Wittgenstein became an old friend and Akhenaten became an even older friend. Conversely, Richard Dawkins became a sparring mate and Sigmund Freud became an absolute punching bag.

You were convinced that limits were meant exclusively for calc—a class you had already completed, and would probably never revisit. Even then, though, the limit did not always exist.

You knew that the world would never change without a catalyst, and at seventeen, you were gearing up to become one. Here's hoping you've held on to your drive, your joie de vivre, and your otherworldly collection of highlighters along the way. (Pro tip: using multiple different highlighters to color-code annotations is life changing, tbh.)

I look forward to meeting you someday, Amanda—I'm sure you'll be making us both proud.

Ta-ta for now,
Amanda Mickelson, 17

Find Your Passion

EVERY DAY I'M HUSTLING

LATICIA ROLLE

Laticia has opted for a less direct path to success, oftentimes shunning the advice of family and friends to pursue her own goals. Learning that corporate jobs weren't the path for her, she pursued her dream of modeling and is now the successful owner of BluHazl. com, a fashion and lifestyle blog. She is living the life she imagined and is willing to work hard to make it all happen.

Dear Twenty-Something Self,

I know you are experiencing a lot of anxiety right now and you have no clue what to do, where you want to go, or what exactly you want to be. You are trying your best to make it in Miami following your dreams. Although **your dreams are causing you to work harder than ever** and you're constantly facing tribulations in the modeling industry due to your height, don't quit.

You were taught never to give up, and for that I'm proud of you.

You will make it—just keep going!

I know at times it feels like your other jobs are exhausting, but your hustle and determination allows you to have an awesome beach apartment right on Miami Beach where you will create endless memories with incredible people. **So keep up that hustle and work hard** because **in order to live the life you want,** you have to achieve that—**nobody is going to hand it to you.** You got this, stay positive!
At times, I know your family may not understand why you chose to work in the modeling industry after just graduating with a business degree, but remember this is your dream and this is your life. You have to live it for you. So this new job at the law firm that you hate, that you got solely to please your dad, stop. You need to do what makes you happy, not do what makes others happy.

Some people might not always understand your journey, but trust me: **listen to your heart and your mind will follow.** I'm proud of you for quitting that job and going to model overseas in South Africa for three months after everyone said not to. **Way to take a risk, girl!** Way to follow your heart!

Now that you've followed your heart, you're in a different continent by yourself with no family or friends, your anxiety level is out of control.

You're on a new journey, chasing your dreams and about to meet lifelong friends. Don't be shy, open up. **Say hi more and smile always,** because you're about to have the time of your life in South Africa with your best friend, Codie. Skype Mom and Dad weekly and let them know you're doing great. You're booking jobs regardless of your height and exploring this beautiful world. Look at you! They're still so proud of you. You're doing it, girl! You're living!

All my best,
Laticia

Find Your Passion

TRANSFORM STRESS for GOOD

DR. HEIDI HANNA

Dr. Hanna is founder and Chief Energy Officer of Synergy, a consulting company providing brain-based health and performance programs for organizations; the Executive Director of the American Institute of Stress; and a frequent lecturer at Canyon Ranch Resort and Spa in Tucson, AZ. Dr. Hanna's publications include the NY Times Best-Seller The SHARP Solution: A Brain-Based Approach for Optimal Performance *(Wiley, Feb 2013),* Stressaholic: 5 Steps to Transform Your Relationship With Stress *(Wiley, Jan 2014), and* Recharge: 5 Shifts to Energize Your Life *(Synergy, 2015). Her next book,* What's So Funny About Stress, *is expected to be released in 2017.*

1. Get clarity on what you're really feeling.

Most people use the word stress as a catch-all for anything that's bad, which provides no way to understand or change the situation. Are you overwhelmed? Tired? Stretched too thin? Do you feel rushed? Isolated? Sad? You can't manage what you can't measure. Stop, assess the situation, and figure out what's at the root of your pressure, tension, or worry so you can make progress.

WOWsdom! The Girl's Guide to the Positive and the Possible   129

2. Take imperfect action.

Even if you can't fix the problem, doing something that gives you a sense of progress not only mobilizes the stress hormones that turn harmful if left too long to wreak havoc on the body, but also boosts your confidence in knowing you can do something about it. When we feel out of control, stress can become paralyzing. But when we start to move, it enables us to use the energy of stress to fuel positive change. **Take time to celebrate the little wins along the way and each one will lead to even greater gains.**

3. Notice what's already going well.

Because of the brain's negativity bias, **we often get stuck thinking about what's wrong and miss all the good things about life. The more we look for positive,** the more we experience positive, and we actually train our brain to create a more resilient lens through which to see the world around us. Before you try to make a course correction to solve your stress, shift into a more optimal brain state by reflecting on something or someone you are grateful for. This actually triggers the release of brain chemicals that will enhance your ability to create new solutions.

4. Do something fun or funny.

Get outside, play with a pet, watch a funny movie. **Sometimes we just need to shift our state of being in order to change our state of mind.** If possible, incorporate physical activity to trigger the release of positive chemicals in the brain and body that will boost your mood. **Call a friend and laugh out loud.** Finding something funny reduces stress hormones and helps boost the creative part of your brain to problem solve more effectively.

5. Help someone else.

Research has shown that the greatest boost in mood comes from helping someone else. Whether it's a random act of kindness to a stranger, sending a hand written card to a friend or family member, or volunteering in the community, **when we provide support for others, we not only let go of our worries for a while, we also boost nourishing brain chemicals like oxytocin that help us heal** from the wear and tear of the daily grind. Knowing we're contributing to kindness also helps us feel more connected and can enhance self-esteem.

Find Your Passion

AD ASTRA*

TAYLOR RICHARDSON

Taylor, also known as Astronaut StarBright, is fourteen years old and has aspirations of becoming a scientist, engineer, and an astronaut one day. She is an advocate, activist, speaker, and philanthropist, most recently raising over $20,000 to send girls to screenings of Hidden Figures, *a film about the women who helped launch our space program. After speaking to over 100,000 people at the March for Science in Washington, D.C., she was featured in the 2017 list of* Teen Vogue's 21 under 21.

Dear Future Taylor,

Congratulations on all the progress you've made! You love that you are inspiring, engaging, and leading girls to the STEM table. **You have helped thousands of girls all over the world to DREAM STEM BIG and pay it forward through service as well.** You are showing girls, especially black girls, that they can be anything they want to be: an astronaut, an engineer, a scientist, a mathematician, or even the president of the United States!

You love how you have been able to ask for and receive guidance and support from mentors in your life who are committed to helping you become the highest version of yourself. You love that you feel at home in the skin that you're in, **because your Black is Beautiful and it ROCKS!** You love the way you keep showing up for yourself and for your purpose, even when it feels uncomfortable and scary. You no longer are interested in centering those who refuse to see your humanity. You lean into your own power and speak your truth. You don't work to prove your humanity to others; you work because the humanity of others gives you strength.

You love the young woman you are becoming because she is more courageous, confident, and self-aware than ever before. Your life is much better now and it's all because of your hard work and dedication. You are beautiful. You are powerful. You are worthy. Your life matters. You were never put on this earth to be a clone but to be your own. **You are the sole author of the dictionary that defines you and there are blank pages still to be written!!**

Ad astra! Love, Taylor.

*To the Stars

FAILURE IS AN OPTION

LARRAINE SEGIL

Originally from South Africa, Larraine sits on the boards of public and private companies; is CEO of The Little Farm Company, a Los Angeles-based family holding company; an Adjunct Professor at two universities; and writes songs for her grandchildren, published on rockingrandmamusic.com. She has always had an eye for moving forward, despite whatever adversity may present itself. Her selfless pursuit of paying it forward has lead to Larraine Segil Scholars—endowed scholarships with an emphasis on mentorship.

Dear eighteen-year-old self:

Since your dad died, you feel very insecure. Life without your anchor—he was only 56—seems unthinkable. And since your mom was so ill, you always thought she would pass first. **Losing a parent changed your life forever. Now it is time to move forward.**

You have so much intelligence and ability and all you have to do is to give it time and life will evolve to give you all the chances that you have studied so hard to make happen.

Go for every opportunity. **Failure is acceptable. In fact, if you don't try hard enough, you will achieve none of your dreams and so you have to be prepared to fail.** What do you do when you fail? You think about the lessons learned and pick yourself up and go forward.

What you don't know is that the future will be one where you will achieve your dreams and immigrate to the country of your dreams—the United States of America. You have thought about that opportunity since you were seven years old and saw the yearbooks of your neighbors who were Americans and you saw young women and men who looked happy and free and full of future opportunities. That is what you want now and you will get it. You will live in a country where people are free, where women CAN achieve whatever they set their hearts on, where the natural answer to questions is "YES," not "NO." It will all happen—not in a linear straight line—but with the normal ups and downs of life.

There will be enormously hard work in your future, lots of examinations, lots of studying while others are playing, staying indoors with your books while others swim at the beach or in the pool—but it will pay off.

And then you can do what you always dreamed of—pay it forward and give back to other women. Be confident, secure, upbeat, and positive—and hold your faith in the future and your abilities and that you will love and will be loved. Take care of your body—you will be challenged with many health issues over the next many decades and your attitude, energy, and determination will enable you to overcome all of it and your later years will be your healthiest, your happiest, and the time for peace of mind and philanthropy.

Always forward,
Larraine

> Leadership is about the decisions you make and the action that you take each day. The world is waiting. Leadership is a choice—and it starts with you.
> —Alyse Nelson, Vital Voices

AMBITION
LOOKS GOOD on You!

KELLY WALLACE

Talk about having a dream job! Kelly is a digital correspondent and editor-at-large for CNN, focusing on family, career, and work/life balance. Getting to her dream job meant taking a lot of knocks along the way—and separating herself from the pack with dogged determination and trust in herself. Kelly is also a great mom to two energetic and wonderful daughters.

To My Younger Self,

Be bold. Take chances. Don't worry about what other people think. Stop apologizing. Raise your hand even when you aren't sure you have the correct answer. Go for the job even when you aren't sure you have all the qualifications required.

Be curious. Ask a ton of questions. And be confident. Know you've got this.

When your body seems to change overnight, don't be afraid and upset. Love yourself for who you are inside and out. **And know there will be a day when you truly feel comfortable in your own skin.**

When you go to college at sixteen and suddenly realize you are a lot younger than everyone else, know the first months will be rough but don't let other people question whether you belong there. You do.

When you graduate from college and many of your classmates are headed to lucrative Wall Street positions and you are struggling to find an entry-level job in the news industry, don't worry. You will find one.

When the rejection letters pile up as you pursue your dream of becoming an on-air reporter, don't worry. You only need one offer. And be sure to save those rejection letters. They will be fun to look at when you make it.

When a male supervisor criticizes you—by asking, "Why are you so ambitious?"—don't question yourself and wonder whether you are doing anything wrong. YOU AREN'T. You are just going for what you want. If a man did that, he would be applauded, not challenged.

When another male supervisor takes issue when you are pushing for a bigger part of the coverage of a story, realize he probably wouldn't question you if you were a man.

AND NEVER APOLOGIZE FOR ASKING FOR MORE.

And while you are working so much and so hard, find time to breathe. To enjoy a sunrise on a summer day. The first snowfall of the winter. A plunge into the ocean. A good book. A day with your girlfriends. A long phone call with your mom. A lunch with that young producer who keeps asking you out. (He will eventually become your husband, best friend, and partner in raising two dynamic young women.)

Because you will see how fast it all goes, savor every moment of the journey. And take time to pat yourself on the back. To feel proud of everything you have accomplished. How far you have come. And then pay it forward whenever you can. Make time to help other young women who are trying to get ahead, because when more women succeed, we all benefit.

I'm so proud of you.
Kelly

THE BOSSY GIRL SYNDROME

I want every little girl who someone says, "They're too bossy," to be told instead, "You have leadership skills," because I was told that and because every woman I know who's in a leadership position was told that.
—Sheryl Sandber

Sheryl Sandberg, the Chief Operating Officer of Facebook and author of the best-selling book *Lean In*, launched "Ban Bossy" in 2014 as a way to encourage girls to pursue leadership roles.

From banbossy.com:

When a little boy asserts himself, he's called a "leader." Yet when a little girl does the same, she risks being branded "bossy." Words like bossy send a message: don't raise your hand or speak up. By middle school, girls are less interested in leading than boys—a trend that continues into adulthood. Together we can encourage girls to lead.

BAN BOSSY'S TOP 10 TIPS FOR GIRLS:

1. Speak up in class

2. Stop apologizing before you speak

3. Challenge yourself

4. Ask for help

5. Don't do everyone else's work

6. Speak up in friendship

7. Trust your inner voice

8. Change the world

9. It's not always easy to speak up, but it's worth it

10. Practice!

Sandberg, Sheryl. "Leadership Tips for Girls." Ban Bossy, 10 March 2014, www.banbossy.com/girls-tips, brought to you by LeanIn.org and Girl Scouts of the USA

DO YOU BELIEVE IN MAGIC?

Believing in magic is not believing in some made up kind of thing. It's believing in the power you have to go after the life you see in your dreams.

Believing in magic doesn't ignore the hard stuff that comes with living; instead it's the fuel that keeps you going even when times get tough. I know all too well about the hard stuff in life, and I also know it was the belief in my own magic that kept me rising. As I did during the tough times, focus on what you can control including how you care for your MIND, BODY, and SPIRIT.

What are some ways that you can keep YOUR magic alive in these three areas:

MIND: _____

BODY: _____

SPIRIT: _____

ATIYA ABDELMALIK, MSN, RN

Atiya is passionate about helping women and girls live their best lives and as Executive Director—and Main Magician—for Generation WOW she is doing just that. For more than twenty years, Atiya has enjoyed a diverse career as a nurse, health promotion director, and community engagement leader. Atiya believes each one of us has WOW magic, the kind that can transform lives and transform communities. Atiya enjoys fulfilling roles as a wife, mother, and dogmommy to Nemo and Dory.

ARMOR FOR LIFE

With all that life has coming at you, self care and even a little extra self love can be wonderful armor for life, work, and sport. I use movement and eating well as the easiest form of therapy to keep my mind right. Yes, I used to really only think about performance on the court and now I think about performance in life and for the long run. As a 6'3" woman, the first thing I decided to do was to do my best to accept who I am and not to try and fit in to some mold of what I am supposed to be. Cute and size two wasn't in my cards so what were my aces? I always say we all get dealt low and high cards, so play your high cards.

A FEW SIMPLE TIPS TO ACHIEVE BETTER HEALTH:

① Sleep is King

The best way recover from the day's activity is to get to bed. Develop a solid sleep hygiene practice, so turn off your computer, create a dark cool space, and get to bed.

② Simply Drink Water

Americans consume 20% of their calories in what they drink, so why not stick to the good stuff? Not to mention we are all dehydrated, which is disruptive to your health. Get hydrated and help your skin, elimination, and body processes. Did I say skin?

Find Your Passion

③ Eat Real Food

It's simple: do your best to consume food that is as close to the source as possible. If it can live in a bag for three years or has a bunch of ingredients you don't recognize, just pass.

④ move that gift of yours called your BODY.

It is not necessary to kill yourself each day, but find something you can do on a consistent basis and schedule into your life like everything else. Try to get your heart rate up two to three times a week, and change it up from time to time. Your body is smart and will adapt.

⑤ Customize your Life.

However you eat, move, meditate, or even have fun, do it YOUR way. There is no one size fits all so invest a little time to figure out what truly works best for you.

Here's to your health.

Aloha, Gabby Reece

GABRIELLE REECE

A champion on and off the court, Gabby is not only a volleyball legend but an inspirational leader who demonstrates wit, candor, and sheer motivation. Her intense passion and dedication to health and fitness has led her to become a dominant influencer in this highly sought after space. Together with her husband, surfing legend Laird Hamilton, Gabby is an avid proponent of empowering people to take responsibility for their own health and has become a role model to women worldwide regarding how to achieve peak fitness, good health, and overall well-being for themselves and their entire family.

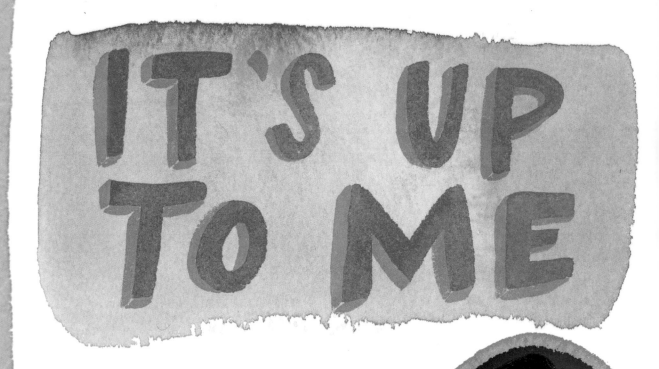

DR. CHRISTYL JOHNSON

Dr. Christyl Johnson joined NASA's Goddard Space Flight Center in Maryland as Deputy Center Director for Technology and Research Investments in December 2010. She came to NASA Goddard from the White House Office of Science and Technology Policy and she formerly served under the President's Science Advisor as the Executive Director of the National Science and Technology Council. Dr. Johnson is a well-respected speaker and supporter of girls and women in STEM.

As a woman you need to understand that you bring a unique perspective to the table. **There is power in your uniqueness, and you can use it to your advantage to offer solutions that others may not even think about based on their life experiences.** Own that uniqueness!! Use it to make this world a better place!! If you don't believe in yourself, and the talent that you bring to the table, how can you expect others to believe in you? Know who you are and what you bring to the table, and don't let anyone else's view of you change that. No one can tell you what is possible for you and what is not. No one can realize your dreams but you, and no one can stop you from achieving them BUT YOU! Always remember...

...IT'S UP TO ME.

When I was in my first year of college, I had to complete a summer internship at a NASA center as a part of my scholarship. When I was told that I was assigned to a physics lab, I was quite disappointed because I had no idea how physics could lead to any kind of career I would be interested in. Well I must say, working in that laser lab that summer changed my life for the better! Because of the unique vantage point of girls and women, we can use our ingenuity and creativity to solve so many of the challenges that face our world.

Over my career, I have seen women use careers in Science, Technology, Engineering, and Math to provide medical breakthroughs; design better cars, airplanes, trains, and other vehicles; launch vehicles and payloads into space; create amazing special effects for movies; develop lifesaving equipment to rescue people from traumatic accidents; and countless other ground-breaking achievements to improve the quality of everyday life for all of us.

If you allow yourself to dream and don't give in to fear, who knows what YOU will discover, where YOU will go, who YOU will help, and how YOU WILL CHANGE THE WORLD!!

FOOD
FOR THOUGHT

LONNIE ALI

After her marriage to boxing and civil rights legend Muhammad Ali in November 1986, Lonnie and her husband opened the Muhammad Ali Center in Louisville in November 2005, where she serves as a Lifetime Director and as Vice Chair of the Center's Board. Lonnie has been active in various charitable causes including advocating for children's rights and Parkinson's disease research. From 2010 to 2013, Lonnie served on President Obama's Commission for the Study of Bioethical Issues.

Dear Lonnie,

You did it! Graduation day is finally here, and you've worked hard. You've been diligent about planning your life from fifth grade until now. You've been careful and at times even fretted over getting to this day. And although you are over the moon with excitement, you are anxious about what tomorrow will bring.

Don't worry about tomorrow; for the most part it will take care of itself. **Don't obsess.** Whatever happened in the past can't be changed—it's over. Don't carry it forward and allow it to overshadow today. **You have today. Live it. Savor it.**

You've made plans, though nothing is certain. Graduate school is a possibility; then there is that great job offer you got from that consumer brands company. Your mind is in a tizzy trying to figure it all out—what is the right decision? This is the beginning of the rest of your life and you know whatever you decide will put you on a life path that will impact you in some way, every day. **What could be more important?**

Understandably, right now you're filled with uncertainty. Remember that your chances of success are good with either choice you make, and life is not much of a success if you don't learn to enjoy while you're living it.

> ## To really enjoy life, you must get out of your head, AND LIVE IN THE MOMENT.

You know that thing you have for helping other people plan their lives because you like facilitating success for others, too? **Remember not everyone thinks like you.** I know you want to help—be patient and wait until you're asked. And when you are, don't go overboard with the advice. Don't grow up and be a helicopter mom, hovering over your children to see what they will do. Like you, **people, including your children, will take what they need and leave the rest.** Give them that opportunity. If you don't, you'll be wasting valuable energy trying to change their way of thinking. Instead, **refocus that energy on making "you" the best you can be.**

Speaking of energy, as you go through life, don't forget to be conscious and aware of the people around you who are in real need. Use some of your valuable energy to help others; preferably before they're forced to ask you for that help. **Look for daily opportunities to perform acts of kindness and service—big and small. It feeds your soul.** Acts of service are calorie free—you're free to perform as many as you want every day of your life. These precious and personal insights are "food for thought" as you live your life to the fullest.

Be great and do great things!

All my love,

Me

LIVE YOUR

PURPOSE

To make a difference, to change the WORLD, to be purposeful in a passionate way, creates positivity where all things become possible.

PRACTICE COURAGE

GISELLE CARSON

Giselle is the walking definition of a powerhouse—a highly respected immigration attorney and, as an immigrant herself, she is paying it forward. She is a four-time Ironman Finisher, including the Big One in Kona, Hawaii; a member of the Seven Continent Marathon Club; and she recently completed all six world major marathons (Boston, Chicago, New York, London, Berlin, and Tokyo). She is trilingual and married to Jeff, a physical therapist, marathon runner, and triathlete.

Dear Fifteen-Year-Old Giselle,

Right now, you're feeling scared, uncertain, and more than a little angry. You thought this was a family trip to Czechoslovakia. A once-in-a-lifetime experience outside of Cuba. Two short weeks to celebrate becoming a quinceañera.

But now you're in Montreal. And the plane to Czechoslovakia went on without you. Your parents say you won't go back to Cuba. Ever. This isn't a family trip; it is an escape from the Castro regime. This sinks in.

You will never see your friends again. Your language, your culture, and your home are gone forever. A determination fills your heart. Your parents are wrong. So wrong. You are not staying here. You will find your way back.

Hold on to that determination. It will serve you well. But that desire to go back to live in Cuba will diminish, though your love for your culture will remain strong.

This change is scary. Change always is. But this move will open new opportunities.

In Cuba, you envisioned marrying and starting a family. You'd finish your bachelor's, but you have no idea what you'd do with it. You wouldn't get to choose your career.

That's all changed now. You have control over your future in a whole new way.

What if I told you that you'll design your own career in two different fields that excite you? That you'll build a team that you lead? Run many marathons?

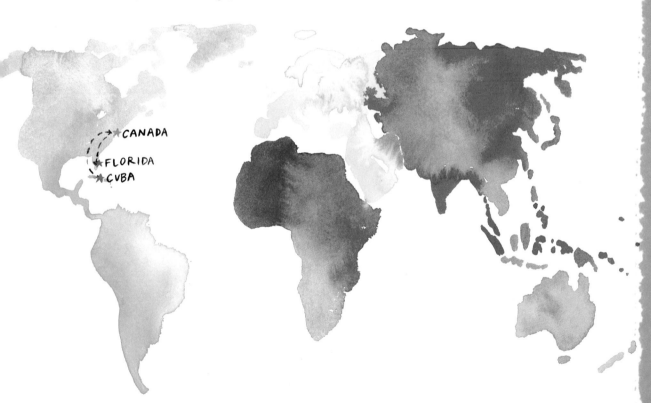

Visit all seven continents?

CANADA

FLORIDA

CUBA

Adjusting to new cultures and learning two new languages won't be easy. It will be overwhelming and lonely at times. **But pay attention to what you learn on that journey. You'll revisit those lessons again,** sooner than you expect.

Eventually, Canada feels like home. You go to physical therapy school where you meet and fall in love with Jeff, an *extranjero* (foreigner) who will change your destiny. You join a growing number of interracial married couples. Together, you embrace physical fitness and your careers.

Anything seems possible—you have big goals—but something feels missing.

You take several vacations to Florida, and you find it: your Cuban family and culture you lost. There, they are supportive and vibrant. You and Jeff make a radical decision: you leave behind everything you know in Canada. And, once again, the change is scary.

But courage takes practice; the SECOND time is easier than the FIRST

In your first few years in Florida, you make friends, buy your first house, get your first dog, and continue to work as a physical therapist. When Jeff decides to pursue his doctorate, you re-evaluate your career and decide you want to make a greater impact.

After much research, you collect your courage and apply to law school. You get in! You're thrilled...but also terrified. It's change again. You're leaving your old field behind...and entering the unknown.

Attending law school part-time while working full-time as a physical therapist makes for long, long days. But eventually you graduate–first in your class! All that hard work paid off. You combine your past medical knowledge with your new law degree and work as a medical malpractice defense attorney.
But it doesn't feel right. Your passion is elsewhere. You remember how grateful you felt for the immigration attorneys in Canada and then in the U.S. Their work and guidance enabled you to achieve you dreams. You want to do the same for others, so you dive into change yet again.

Today, you have a successful business immigration practice helping employers hire and retain foreign nationals. Every day, you and your team work to help people uproot and change their lives for the better. Like you are doing at just fifteen today in that Canadian airport.

Live Your Purpose

CULTIVATING COURAGE

"It takes courage to grow
up and become who you really are."
—e. e. cummings

Embrace
Your Dreams:
Live Them
Out Loud

Face Your Fears:
Say Them
Out Loud

Drink In Your
New Successes
and Repeat

Gather Allies:
Make Real Friends

Move Forward:
One Step at a Time

Oh, dear Giselle–

CHANGE IS SCARY
But you can do more than you think you can!

Be courageous! We each have about 80,000 working hours in a lifetime. You won't be able to do it all in life. Pick the things you really want to do. Surround yourself with people who can guide you. And go make it happen!

Don't forget to appreciate the people who help you; pay it forward. And take time to appreciate your wins—big and small.

As you watch that plane fly away without you today, you feel as though your life is ending. But it's barely begun!

Sincerely,
Your Future Self

LIVE, LEARN, LEAD TOGETHER

Immigrant (n)—a person who comes to live permanently in a foreign country.

The United States of America is a country of immigrants. Giselle tells her story of "escaping" from Cuba to arrive in the U.S.; Ita's parents (see pg. 152) were able to move here from Nigeria; and then there is Larraine's dream to leave South Africa. Donna's grandparents are from Russia and Poland. Sabeen (pg. 176) came to the U.S. via Pakistan. Some families escaped to America, fleeing war and strife; others were forcibly brought to America as slaves; and others had the good fortune to choose to come to America.

In the first two hundred years in America, fewer than one million immigrants (mostly British and French) came to the U.S. from Europe. In 1780—four years after the signing of the Declaration of Independence—our country had 2.78 million citizens. Today, we are a melting pot of over 308 million people and nearly 14 million immigrants entered the U.S. between 2000 and 2010 from all corners of the globe.

Today, we continue welcoming people, and invariably someone you know or their parents or grandparents came from somewhere else.

Where is your family from? _____

How did they get here? _____

What is your favorite cultural tradition? _____

Take the time to talk to your friends and neighbors and ask them about their family's cultural experience and journey to America. No matter where our families originate, our histories and cultures add so much richness to each others lives. Learning to appreciate and respect the diversity of our country will lead us to innovate and imagine more for ourselves and our neighbors.

GIVING You THE BEST That I GOT

ITA EKPOUDOM

Ita grew up the child of Nigerian immigrants—no easy feat in the American South. With an intense focus on education and achievement, Ita went on to receive her MBA from the prestigious Wharton School at the University of Pennsylvania. That drive continues today as Ita works through her company, Tigress Ventures, to engage, educate, and elevate the next generation of successful female business leaders and investors.

Dear Teenage Me,

I remember you well. In fact, it doesn't feel that long ago that I WAS you (and sometimes I still feel I AM you even though the calendar says otherwise!) I remember you so fondly because during that time you represented some of the best aspects of me that, quite frankly, I need to channel again.

First, I remember you so fondly because you were surrounded by the people who loved you most, your family. It's hard to tell you this, but today your mom, dad, and sister are no longer here with us. We no longer hear their words of encouragement and laughter (and even those eye roll worthy, "Where are the other 3 points?" when you brought home a 97% on a test.) **Treasure every moment with your** family. You will never have stronger and louder cheerleaders in your corner who will love you unconditionally. Whenever possible, tell them that you love them and let them know that you appreciate their love.

Second, because of the wonderful parents we had, we were so lucky to grow up in a wonderful community, despite being black foreigners living in the Deep South. I know how crafty you were, getting involved in school to help you get out from under the rules of our very strict parents because for them doing well academically came above all else. I commend you for that! I remember how upset you were when you ran for student council president in the fourth grade and lost. And how you pulled back a bit then, because who enjoys losing?

But you knew that your ticket out of the house in middle school and high school was to get involved. So you started playing sports and learning what it meant to be a good teammate on and off the field. The friendships you made and confidence you gained on those teams helped you feel emboldened to try again and run for class president freshman year of high school, working with a couple of your close female friends and classmates to campaign together. I am glad you were naïve enough to believe you SHOULD run and COULD win. And thanks to teachers and classmates who believed in us, the three of you DID WIN. And by working together and LISTENING to the issues that mattered to all of your classmates and not just a few, you all got re-elected all four years.

> "I think togetherness is a very important ingredient to family life."
>
> —Barbara Bush,
> First Lady of the United States, 1989–1993

Can you send me, your older self, that unbridled optimism and belief that I can make a difference? Can you give me the courage to try to work with my fellow peers again to build a sense of spirit in my community today? I think looking at you then is teaching me so much more that I should be using today. So thank you for seeking positivity and the good in those around you, and I hope that I can do my best to draw from that and not let you down.

Love,
Your Thirty-Something Self

Journalist and author Jay Newton-Small, when writing of women in government, said, "Women are the only ones in Washington who still do business the old-fashioned way: by forging relationships and fostering trust." Newton-Small also noted that when female representation is "somewhere between twenty percent and 30 percent, women really begin to change an institution, whether it's a legislature or a corporate board, a Navy ship or an appellate court."

Read more about the role of women in the 2016 book,
Broad Influence: How Women Are Changing the Way America Works.

Pay It Forward

We all stand on the shoulders of those have come before us. People have given much of their time, their hearts, and their resources to make others' lives better. We all have that opportunity and responsibility, as Larraine Segil says. One good deed a day is one of the best things we can do for others and ourselves. Like Dr. Heidi Hana says, "Research has shown that the greatest boost in mood comes from helping someone else."

Pick something—or a few things—to focus on each day. Even one small act is enough to be life-changing for someone else and yourself. Add your own ideas to the list!

- Smile at someone you don't know

- Carry someone's grocery bags

- Give up your seat for someone who could make use of it

- Say "thank you" often

- Pick up trash when you see it

- Give someone an honest compliment

- Become someone's mentor

- Read to younger children

- Volunteer with an organization

- Pay the animal shelter a visit

- Be a helper

- Raise your hand and say YES

BETTER LATE THAN NEVER

CINDY EDELMAN

An active community volunteer, Cindy's life has been rooted in service to others. Whether as a high school AP Art History instructor or a founding member of the Holocaust Memorial Museum in Washington, D.C., Cindy's passion for learning and education has made a her a difference-maker and permeates every conversation and every endeavor. A founder of the Jacksonville Public Education Foundation, her commitment to community has lead to many awards and board positions focused on youth and education.

Hey Greener,

Being a late bloomer has turned out not to be such a bad thing! But why did you always have to be so stubborn? Why didn't you listen to Dad when he advised you to get your teacher's certificate in college, instead of at forty?

Here is my list of best advice for you—in no particular order:

Develop your mind! Read and study and find a field that speaks to you. Stick with it and become the best you can be, whether art history teacher or gift buyer.

Make the most of your education; it is really your ticket to freedom, and while you are at it, **avoid debt.** It is so easy to get into debt but so hard getting out.

Develop your body. Now I know shopping isn't exactly an athletic endeavor, but exercise has some very positive benefits, including being fit, looking well, and all those endorphins that bring peace of mind. After running four marathons, it is thrilling to know that you have it in you to push yourself, and your sense of accomplishment is extraordinary.

Expand your heart to allow those who are different than you in; there is so much to learn from others.

> ## "As I give, I get."
> —Mary McLeod Bethune, founder of the Daytona Normal and Industrial Institute in 1904, which later became Bethune-Cookman College (an HBCU).

Serve, Serve, Serve others. Volunteer, mentor, tutor; there are always people who are worse off than you. There is nothing better than giving to others, nothing, because a life of service is a life full of unexpected rewards.

Finally, learn to recognize and appreciate the beauty around you, whether a gorgeous sunset, a delicate flower, a dance, a Monet or Van Gogh painting, or musical composition, train yourself to be aware of all the beauty in the world, and be one who looks for the positive in life. That will steel you as you face adversity.

All my best,
Cindy

Recognizing and appreciating the beauty around us.

What are three beautiful things around you now? Can you do this with your eyes closed as well?

1. _____

2. _____

3. _____

> "I felt my lungs inflate with the onrush of scenery—air, mountains, trees, people. I thought, 'This is what it is to be happy.'"—Sylvia Plath, The Bell Jar

COMMUNITY ENGAGEMENT

NINA WATERS

Nina Waters has led Florida's oldest and largest community foundation since 2005. During her tenure, the Foundation's assets and annual grant-making have quadrupled, with total assets of $343 million and annual grants to the community of $43 million at the end of 2016. Nina's accomplishments include the launch of a ten-year Quality Education for All Initiative and the development of the Foundation's first giving circle, the Women's Giving Alliance.

Have you ever heard someone say, "The whole is more than the sum of its parts?" It means that when you join with others, you can accomplish much more than working by yourself. Don't miss the opportunity to get involved with others in your community, and make sure you ask them to join you!

When you see change that needs to happen or a need that must be addressed, reach out to find others who can help you achieve your goal. Each of you will bring your individual strengths to an effort, and the combined energy of your group often means a superior outcome. Often, you'll learn a new way to look at a problem or a different perspective on an issue—those can often help you in your search for a solution.

And be sure to look outside the normal borders of your day-to-day activities—enlist others who may look or think differently from you or come from a different way of life. Whatever you are working on will benefit by including a diverse set of opinions and expertise. Most of all, by embracing others in your area that want to see change and improvement, you will be making your community one that is more closely knit, more inclusive, and more reflective of the people who live there.

you may be thinking— how do I begin?

Social media platforms have so many tools that can help you engage friends and others with a cause that you care about.

If you're not sure where to get engaged, think about causes that have been important to you in your life —perhaps Girl Scouts, a youth group at your place of worship, the Humane Society, or a health issue that has impacted you or a close family member.

Contact organizations in your community that address one of the causes that are important to you or look on their website for opportunities to volunteer or participate in an upcoming event.

Giving your time is often more valuable to the organization than giving money. And involving others not only multiplies the benefit to those being served by the organization, it also makes the experience more fun!

PROVE YOURSELF RIGHT

GRACE FREEDMAN

Grace is a girl on a mission! Even as a rising junior, she wants to save the world and improve people's lives. As a founding member of the Generation WOW after-school club at Ponte Vedra High School in Ponte Vedra, Florida, Grace's determination, never-ending energy, and purposeful optimism leave no doubt she will impact the world for the better.

Dear Future Self,

I hope that you are passionately fighting against the all-too-prevalent HIV virus and striving to decrease regional disparities in medicine. Hopefully you will be successful. Not too long ago, you were dreaming up ways to help the developing world and those in it, and now look where you are. **Please call Dad whenever you get the chance and thank him** for his invaluable efforts to push you to be the best you possibly could be. I guess the countless hours of AP chemistry and ACT prep will pay off in the long run. After all, he always knew you were the diamond, no matter how many times you thought of yourself as lost in the rough. Also, when you get into the school of your choice, tell him I told you so. You've always valued respect and understanding and I hope that still holds true today.

My wish is that you've traveled far and wide, immersing yourself in different cultures and learning about the world we live in. I know for a fact that you will someday make it to the Louvre and admire the artwork for days. Remember, Grace: always keep your head up and that the best revenge is to improve

Live Your Purpose

yourself. The world is changed by your example, not your opinion, so when you want something done, get up and get it done. Silence is, after all, the real crime against humanity. You are a strong, intelligent, and capable woman who can handle anything thrown your way. **Oh, and I really do hope that you are part of the movement that puts an end to sexism. I'm tired of the countless double standards and cultural norms that women face, and by the time you are reading this, I wish that you have already done something about it.**

Silence is, after all, the real crime against humanity.
—Grace Freedman, 2016

I am positive you can change people's lives, from ridding the earth of world hunger to obliterating AIDS and HIV. You will truly affect millions of peoples' lives in a positive way. I know that your life will be busy and at times frantic, but **do reserve times to talk to Mom.** She has always been your backbone, personal assistant, and nurturer throughout the years and **you owe her the world.** How's my sister Hope? My bet is that she's changing the world with her smile and her warm heart. Hopefully, over the years your friendship has grown rock solid and you two are inseparable. No matter how many petty arguments you two have had, you guys have never stopped loving each other. If there is anything I have learned in the fifteen years of my existence, it's that **love conquers all.** Use your compassion to change the world of global health and don't stop until you have achieved your goal. Stand tall, speak out, and never stop fighting for what you believe in.

Best of wishes,
Grace

Grace, Piper, and Taylor at Generation WOW

There are so many organizations that lead change and focus on health, education, violence against women, or eradicating poverty. Research to find them and then read up on what these organizations do. How do they view their work? Think about how you can speak up for these organizations and the people they serve and not be silent.

HOW WILL YOU CHANGE the WORLD?

FORGET THE CRYSTAL BALL

SAMANTHA ALVES ORENDER

An admitted Type A personality, Sam loves a good plan. She went to a great high school, Stanton College Preparatory in Jacksonville, Florida, got her law degree from the top school in Florida, and thought she had it all figured out. Sam learned that you make a plan, work a plan, and adjust as necessary because you can't predict the future.

Dear High School Self,

I know you just want to be sure that everything will turn out ok, and I'm here to tell you that it will.

I know your biggest fear, so let me just get to it: you won't get into your first choice college, but you'll get into an even better school, and somehow, you'll even find a way to pay for it. The decision to move so far away from home will be hard, but it will open so many doors for you.

Since you're a planner, I can tell you that some things will be just as you think. You'll go to law school and get a good job. You'll live ten minutes from your parents so you can see them all the time, you'll have wonderful friends, you'll love being a mother, and your husband will be your best friend.

But there is so much you can't predict! After falling in love, you'll break up and spend a year apart before getting married. This will be especially confusing since the whole time, you know he's the one.

WHERE DO YOU SEE YOURSELF IN 5 YEARS?

Take a look at your friends. There are three girls from high school who will become your friends for life, and, surprisingly, it's not who you think. But those three, they will be your home base. Make them a priority.

You'll spend too much time trying to figure out what you want to do with your life, but the truth is, there's not just one thing. Turns out you have a short attention span, so just do what feels right at the time.

One thing will lead to another. The next few years are going to be full of so much change. It doesn't feel good when you're in the middle of it, but looking back, it's the situations that were really hard, that you just powered through, that gave you the strength and courage that you have now.

And although I'm starting to see it, neither of us know just what you're going to do with all that courage.

Love,
Your Adult Self

Having goals and objectives will help you focus on what you want to accomplish. Can you name your top three goals? This can include getting into college, the kind of work you would like to do, and/or a special skill you would like to learn.

GOAL 1: _____

How will you get there? _____

GOAL 2: _____

How will you get there? _____

GOAL 3: _____

How will you get there? _____

Share with a teacher, parent, or mentor and talk about
how you can work together to make these goals a reality.

GETTING INTO COLLEGE
IS A SCIENCE NOT AN ART

RICK SINGER

As a father and coach, Rick has seen the stress that the college admissions process can put on a family. As founder of GettingIntoCollege.com, he has spent the past twenty-five years helping students discover their life passion and guiding them along with their families through the complex college admissions maze to set them on a course to excel in life.

Please close your eyes and envision your dream job. Keep your eyes closed and dream about the lifestyle you would like to have.

Go ahead and open your eyes and write both responses in the notes section of your phone. Every day when you wake up and before you go to bed, PLEASE read your prophetic responses in your notes.

To make your dreams come true, attending college is an absolute MUST! However, the process of getting in and the barriers to entry seem insurmountable, but I am going to give you the Secret Sauce to getting into college.

The coach, that's me, gave you a uniform and I wrote you in as a starter in the lineup. What do you do next—that is easy.

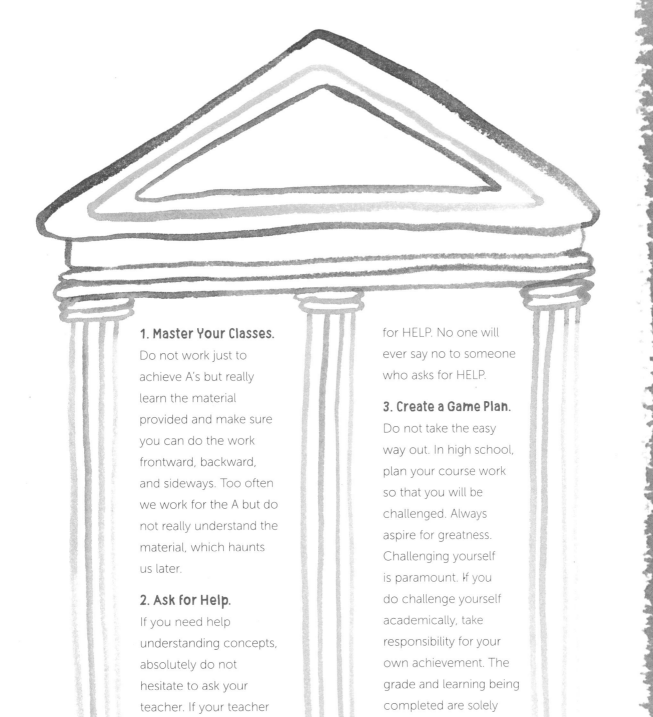

1. Master Your Classes.

Do not work just to achieve A's but really learn the material provided and make sure you can do the work frontward, backward, and sideways. Too often we work for the A but do not really understand the material, which haunts us later.

2. Ask for Help.

If you need help understanding concepts, absolutely do not hesitate to ask your teacher. If your teacher is not responsive, go find another teacher and ask for HELP. No one will ever say no to someone who asks for HELP.

3. Create a Game Plan.

Do not take the easy way out. In high school, plan your course work so that you will be challenged. Always aspire for greatness. Challenging yourself is paramount. If you do challenge yourself academically, take responsibility for your own achievement. The grade and learning being completed are solely your responsibility, not your teachers'!

4. Create a Brand or a Compelling Story.

Getting into college is about showcasing who you are and what you are passionate about. Every college in America wants students who are going to make a difference in the community both in school and out. Never engage in extracurricular activities that you are not passionate about just to have another activity on your resume. Colleges can see through your hyperbole of doing everything just to look better and busy.

5. Never Forget the Five Factors:

Taking the most rigorous courses your school has or the most rigorous courses you can manage—absolutely challenge yourself.

Create a brand or story about yourself. Every college wants to accept you if you can make a difference on or off campus.

Class rank is important, so get the best grades you can from the moment you start high school. If you are already in high school, step up to the plate and work smarter and achieve better grades. It is NEVER TOO LATE to achieve!

Grades—every college recalculates GPA, so you can never get a "plus" on your report card but you should strive for minuses. Yes: a B+ is the same as a B and an A- is the same as an A so always strive for the "minus!"

It's never too early to start preparing for standardized tests (SAT and ACT). Complete a thirty minute section daily. Buy some index cards and write out each math problem missed on the front of the card and the right way to do that problem on the back—practice those you miss every other day and eventually you will memorize how to do every problem on the test.

Lastly, close your eyes again. Envision yourself walking across the stage at your college graduation. Congratulations! You just graduated, it is going to happen if you believe!

~ THOUGHTS on ~
LEADERSHIP

There's a lot of talk about leadership and often we have a clear picture in our mind's eye of what it looks like. I've spent a lot of time trying to figure out the formula for the best kind of leader and here's the obvious conclusion: there is not one. Many of the best leaders I know think big, speak with inspiration, and take charge with ease. These characteristics are easily recognized as LEADERSHIP, but it is often a quieter form, filled with integrity, compassion, empathetic connection, intuition, and inner wisdom that is least seen but deeply felt. **As we go forward in life, we need to listen to our authentic voice (which is sometimes buried deep within) and channel the leader that's real for ourselves.** If you don't lead big and loud, don't fool yourself into thinking that you are not a leader. You may be another breed of leader, who is every bit as powerful...in a very different way.

There is no one formula for leadership. What kind of leader are you?

MELINDA WOLFE

In addition to her corporate career, Melinda exhibits her leadership at a range of non-profits that focus on social justice, reproductive rights, and education. She is a board member of Planned Parenthood of New York City, Auburn Seminary, and Parenthood of New Diversity. Inclusion and the advancement of women are key passions and she has held leadership roles in organizations that support these issues including The Center for Talent Innovation, The National Council for Research on Women, the Women's Forum of NY, and former Mayor Bloomberg's Commission on Women's issues.

FREEDOM LIES IN BEING BOLD!
-ROBERT FROST

MIKHAELA JENNINGS

Mikhaela, a seventeen-year old from PACE Center for Girls in Jacksonville, FL, was featured onstage at Generation WOW in 2015 to read her letter to her future self. PACE Center for Girls provides girls and young women an opportunity for a better future through education, counseling, and advocacy. Having suffered immense loss as a young woman, her dreams for herself are as legendary as her confidence.

Dear Mikhaela,

Your confidence is legendary and I would appreciate it if you would maintain what I've worked since grade school to perfect. I chose to do this letter because I want to look back on these years and be proud of myself. You've lost Grandma and your sister, Khameyea, and **you're still here,** fighting for your happiness. Despite what people believe, **happiness doesn't fall into your lap,** you have to aspire to it.

I want you to stumble upon this letter at twenty-five, hopefully on the rise in your career as a wardrobe stylist. Of course, you would have to discover this in an old box, high up in your storage closet located in your new home in Italy. As you know, that's always been the end game, overseas living after years of travel. I really believe you're well rounded; that's a necessary part of you, or, should I say, us.

I hope you remember what an Ice Princess you were at this seventeen/eighteen cusp. Right now every boy is just moronic to us. When you do decide to "love," please don't settle: go in with the intent to love completely. Keep taking everyone at face value—what they say, how they act—but if they lie and don't show all sides of themselves, you know who you are dealing with. I want you to know I love myself now, and I still love you no matter what mistakes you've made.

Finally, because you know better than anyone, remember, Mikhaela: **Subtlety is for those who lack the skills and heart to be bold!**

With much love,
Mikhaela

BE EXTRA-ORDINARY

What makes you want to get out of bed in the morning? What gets your heart racing and your soul burning with the need to move forward?

Looking for what makes you extraordinary is a life-long journey. You may have the preconceived notion that extraordinary is equal to something grand, beyond your reach, but **becoming extraordinary is a mindset,** an appreciation for the simple things that bring you joy. It is the peace of mind that you have brought something to this earth that only you can bring and the understanding that your path is uniquely your own to follow. One is not born extraordinary, nor do the circumstances in our lives make us extraordinary. **We choose to be extraordinary.** Every day you have the choice of living that day ordinarily or extraordinarily.

Finding your purpose in life, your reason for being on this planet, making the conscious decision to live that purpose every day, is extraordinary. The quest for excellence in all that you do, recognizing that good enough will never be enough, and striving to be more every day than you were the day before sets you on the path to extraordinary. **Recognize the remarkable beauty in all that surrounds you and live**

Live Your Purpose

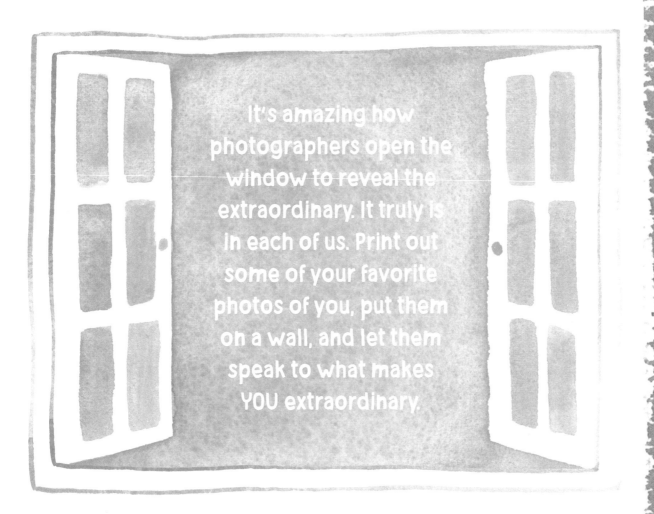

It's amazing how photographers open the window to reveal the extraordinary. It truly is in each of us. Print out some of your favorite photos of you, put them on a wall, and let them speak to what makes YOU extraordinary.

a life of gratitude, not for every breath that you take, but by believing that the next breath will come. Being extraordinary requires you to take risk; throw caution to the wind and live expectant of all of the possible, exciting outcomes. By expanding your vision for the future, challenging the rules, and being willing to follow the path less traveled, you have the opportunity to exceed any imaginable expectation. **Extraordinary people do extraordinary things.**

SUSAN MICHAL

Susan Michal is an internationally published, award winning portrait artist. The first female President of the Professional Photographers of America, Susan specializes in documenting her clients' lives and photographing all of the special moments they want to remember forever.

GO ALL IN

SHERRY LEVIN

Currently the head basketball coach at Worcester Academy in Worcester, MA, Sherry coached the USA Women's Basketball team to a Gold Medal at the 2017 Maccabiah Games in Israel. A Hall of Fame athlete in her own right, Sherry is the consummate team player, whether on the court or off.

Dear Teenage Sherry,

First, let me say **"way to go!"** It has not always been easy to put your head above the crowd. In fact, it can be downright lonely at times. Our parents used to say, **"When you put your head above the crowd, people will try to knock it off."** Somewhat cynical, but true. It's not your fault that some teammates treat you poorly because they are jealous of your success—that is on them. The day you were not voted captain of the basketball team felt like a dagger to the heart. Through the pain and tears, you could not have known that that moment was a defining one for you. You showed up every day determined to be your best and follow the advice of your parents to turn it around and make it a positive life lesson. You find the courage to stay the course and later in life follow your passion of coaching so that you can "make a difference" in the lives of others.

Stay loyal and trustworthy. Continue to befriend those who eat alone or don't seem to have many friends. It comes back to you in spades. Your compassion will continue through life as you mature and then impart that quality to your daughter (yes—you will be blessed with a loving daughter). Loyalty is an amazing quality to have and share with others, which is a reason your close friends have been with you for decades.

Live Your Purpose

BEST ADVICE:
SURROUND YOURSELF WITH POSITIVE-MINDED PEOPLE.

When later on in life you have to deal with the worst kind of adversity—being told those four words, "You have breast cancer"—you keep looking through your positive lens. **Battling cancer was by far the worst ordeal in your life that you had to endure.** By surrounding yourself with like-minded, strong people, your determination and your support system will help you conquer this and create a new lens to help others.

Finally, stay true to who you are—**go "ALL IN" in any endeavor you take on.** Your loving family, amazing experiences, and dear friends build the strong foundation for you.

Love,
Your Future Self

GET OUT THERE and PLAY
GIRLS WHO ARE ACTIVE:

Usually get better grades and have higher graduation rates

Have higher levels of confidence and self-esteem

Have a more positive body image

Learn teamwork and how to persevere

BECOMING a WOMAN of INFLUENCE

SABEEN PERWAIZ

Sabeen, a Pakistani immigrant, is a Community Advocate, the Executive Director of the Florida Nonprofit Alliance, and the Executive Producer of TedXJacksonville. If you met her in person, her poise, confidence, and expertise may make you think Sabeen has a "perfect" life. Sabeen teaches us that travel can heal a lot of wounds—physical and psychic—on your journey to becoming a woman of influence.

Dear Sabeen (16),

You are so much more than you think you are. Right now you don't think you can amount to much more than someone's daughter, wife, or friend.

You are fiercely loyal. I know, it's important. But there are people in your life who help you grow, cheer you on, and push you to be your best. They deserve your loyalty. The others—Who drag you down, make you feel small and weak?—they aren't worth keeping around. Just because you are getting attention from someone does not mean they have the right to make you feel worthless. **Finding your self worth won't be easy.** It will be years before your mind accepts what your heart knows to be true. But the time will come when you wake up and believe in the possibilities that come with each new day, unburdened by the pain of the day before. And when you stop looking back and keep moving forward, you flourish in ways you didn't even think were possible.

I'll tell you what—start by being loyal to yourself. What you are just curious about now will soon become your passion: travel. When you get the opportunity to take that trip abroad without your family—don't waste a minute thinking about it. Exploring Ecuador and the Galapagos Islands for those three weeks, you will discover what it was like to be free from a toxic relationship. And, once you know freedom, you will hold on tightly. You will hike, walk across the equator, see creatures that amaze you, and meet people that inspire you. You will discover yourself and love what you see. What you think is love now isn't the real thing. You were twenty-two years old when he beat you. Landed in the hospital. He constantly told you you were ugly and lucky to be loved–to be grateful for what you have. Remember, you had the courage NOT to believe this.

you learned that TRAVEL is your Real first LOVE

Trust me—travel will teach you what that word means. And it will help heal the wounds of your past.

From where I sit now, your life is one that continues to amaze me. You are well-traveled. You are married. You are a Woman of Influence. You are a convener and a trusted leader.

With love and admiration,
Sabeen

10 SIGNS OF AN UNHEALTHY RELATIONSHIP

These warning signs can help you determine whether you are heading toward a dangerous relationship. While these signs do not guarantee escalation to violence, they are very strong indicators. Ask questions. Educate yourself. Talk about it.

INTENSITY

Rushing the pace of a relationship. Always wanting to see you and talk to you. Feeling like someone is obsessed with you.

JEALOUSY

Getting upset when you text or hang out with people your partner feels threatened by. Accusing you of flirting or cheating. Being possessive over you. Stalking.

MANIPULATION

Convincing you to do things you wouldn't normally feel comfortable with. Ignoring you until they get their way. Using gifts and apologies to influence your decisions.

ISOLATION

Insisting you spend all your time with them. Making you question your own judgement of friends and family. Making you feel dependent on them for money, love, or acceptance.

SABOTAGE

Making you miss work, school, or practice. Talking about you behind your back or starting rumors. Threatening to share private information about you.

BELITTLING

Calling you names. Making rude remarks about who you hang out with, your family, or what you look like. Making fun of you—even if it's played off as just a joke.

GUILTING

Making you feel responsible for their happiness. Making you feel like everything is your fault. Threatening to hurt themselves. Pressuring you to do anything sexual you're not comfortable with.

VOLATILITY

Unpredictable mood swings. Losing control by getting violent or yelling. Threatening to hurt you or destroy things. Making you feel afraid of them.

DEFLECTING RESPONSIBILITY

Blaming you, other people, or past experiences for their actions. Using alcohol or drugs as an excuse. Using mental health issues or past experiences (like a cheating ex or divorced parents) as a reason for unhealthy behavior.

BETRAYAL

Lying to you. Purposely leaving you out or not telling you things. Being two-faced. Acting differently around friends. Cheating while in a relationship with you.

onelove

Founded in 2010 to honor Yeardley Love, One Love works to ensure everyone understands the difference between a healthy and unhealthy relationship. To learn more about Yeardley's story and how you can join the movement to end relationship abuse, please go to joinonelove.org.

DRIVEN TO LEAD

DR. JEFFRIANNE WILDER

Dr. JeffriAnne Wilder has learned to combine her innate sense of leadership with her impressive education to become the Founding Director for the Institute for the Study of Race and Ethnic Relations. She writes, researches, and lectures on the experience of black Americans and other racial/ethnic minorities as a sociologist and scholar at the University of North Florida. JeffriAnne is very passionate about connecting sociology to the every day issues occurring within our society, particularly around women and girls.

Dear Love,

You are more than enough. Take a breath, and take a moment to truly listen to your gut. Hear that inner voice screaming as she rallies you on to accomplish your dreams. Trust and believe that you are not running a race, but rather you are moving to the rhythms of your own purpose-driven path that was made to guide only you.

Pay more attention to that bold voice on the inside that knows you are a leader. You always have been. Remember that day in the second grade? It was the winter of 1984, and you had been patiently waiting all school year for your special day to serve as the class line-leader. In Ms. Smith's class, it was such a momentous occasion for the boys and girls to have their chance to be the leader of the line as the entire class marched from the classroom to the restroom, to the lunchroom, and back. **For a**

second-grader, being the line leader was like being the Grand Marshal of a parade! You had seen many others lead the line, and on many occasions, you had envisioned yourself leading the way for others when it was finally your turn. As quiet and shy as you were, it was your chance to show everyone what a leader you really were.

But as luck would have it, those Ohio winters did not disappoint. You were so devastated that morning as you peered out of your bedroom window to see what seemed like one hundred feet of freshly fallen snow. Your spirit was immediately crushed as you recognized that school would be closed that day and that you would not get your chance to lead the line. Your older siblings mocked you as you cried tears of despair.

I know how heartbroken you were that day, and I know that there have been so many other times that your heart ached from the disappointment and frustration of not being able to lead and to show others what you are really made of. And, my love, let me remind you...

you don't need a special day to TAKE THE LEAD.

You are doing it now. People already see that special light inside of you, and they know that you have a special purpose in this life. You are living it daily. Trust yourself. And know that when it feels like you may have lost your opportunity to shine, you are already sparkling. Much bolder and brighter than you may ever recognize.

To my younger self, my love, don't be so hard on yourself. Know that your time is coming. That time is now, and it will never be too late to chase your wildest dreams.

Lead the way!

Love,
JeffriAnne

PRESS ON, REGARDLESS

MARSHA "MARTY" EVANS

Marty is a retired Rear Admiral in the United States Navy. She didn't have too many female role models while in the service, but that didn't stop her from pressing on. Since her retirement from the Navy, she has served as Executive Director of the Girl Scouts of the USA, President and Chief Executive Officer of the American Red Cross, and was the Interim Commissioner of the LPGA.

Dear Younger Self,

Everyone says it is a crazy idea to suddenly scrap graduate school plans and join the Navy instead. You've always been deliberate and agonized over life decisions, analyzing pros and cons of each possible path. That's good and it has helped you set attainable goals and be successful through your school and college years. This decision is from the heart and will give you valuable experience in stepping off into the truly unknown and stepping up to be part of something larger than yourself and serving others and your country. And it will test your mettle.

As you go off to Navy training, know that you will be challenged in many new ways. The academic part, learning about Naval history and operations, will be easy—you've been in the academic mode for sixteen years. Studying the elements of the Naval profession will set you on a course of continuing professional development. The physical training will be a challenge and you'll not necessarily be the top achiever (perhaps a new experience for you). **If you set fitness goals and put your heart**

into it, you'll be surprised at what you can do. Hopefully, it will establish a lifelong habit of taking care of your body and building stamina for the tough assignments that will come your way.

Professional development and fitness are key elements to your success, but they pale in comparison to the importance of developing your spirit. By that I mean the will to win. Our country is depending on its armed forces to keep us safe. As a Naval officer, you will be a leader of women and men who have volunteered to serve their country, who have made the same commitment you have to go into harm's way if necessary. In the defense of the nation, there is no prize for second place.

> Committing from day one to be the best you can be in the service of your shipmates and the country should be your guidestar.

No matter whether you serve for a couple of years or a full career, you will have a great adventure. Your assignments will be varied, in far-off lands and seas, and no doubt will challenge you in ways you cannot even imagine. Know that your shipmates and your bosses are counting on you and will help you be successful.

GRAND MARSHALL
REAR ADMIRAL
MARSHA J. EVANS
SUPERINTENDENT
NAVAL POSTGRADUATE SCHOOL

Be receptive to mentorship even from your subordinates, especially as a very junior officer. Listen to the lessons from the "old salts." My best advice is some that was given to me by a wonderful Naval officer mentor: **"Press on, regardless."**

Your country is counting on you to serve with honor, courage, and commitment. When you finally take off your uniform and join the ranks of veterans, you will be able to say with great satisfaction, "I served."

Yours in service and love,
Marty

WOMEN COMMITTED TO SERVE

It is only recently (2016) that women were allowed to enlist for all combat positions in the military. Women committed to serve have always contributed, earning their way to lead and take their rightful place shoulder to shoulder with their male counterparts.

1782   Deborah Sampson dresses as a man to serve in General Washington's Army.

1812   Mary Marshall and Mary Allen serve as nurses aboard the USS United States.

1917   Women are allowed to join the military as nurses and support staff.

1948   The Women's Armed Services Integration Act grants women permanent status in the military and entitles them to veteran's benefits.

1976   The first females were admitted to the service academies like West Point and the Naval Academy in Annapolis.

1993   Congress authorizes women to serve on combat ships.

FROM A TO A-MINUS

DR. KATHRYN PEYTON

Dr. Peyton is a firm believer in Winston Churchill's famous line, "If you're going through Hell, keep going." With an undergraduate degree from Stanford University, followed by medical school, Radiology residency, and Breast Imaging fellowship training at the University of California San Francisco; as founder of a non-profit technology company, Mammosphere; a mother; and breast cancer survivor, Dr. Payton knows how to keep going. And sometimes that means going from an A to an A minus.

Dear Fourteen-Year-Old Type-A Self,

As you are inevitably making "to do" lists for the day, week, month—balancing violin practice, homework, sports, clubs, lessons, competitions, orchestras, soccer tournaments, track meets, and your typically over-scheduled day—let me help organize your list to prioritize what's really important!

1) Wake up and do the MIRROR TEST

When you look into the mirror, stop worrying about your hair, your clothes, what other people think. The real "mirror test" is: **do you like who you are? Are you doing your best? Being your kindest? And being true to yourself?** I know you are a compassionate, caring person. But you are more concerned with what other people think and how they react to you and your efforts. If they are grumpy, you think you must have done something to cause that. If you do not receive immediate praise for your work, you feel sad. All wrong! It took me years to figure out that Disney's Seven Dwarfs are simply the personalities of people you come across (Grumpy, Happy, Dopey, Bashful, Sneezy, Sleepy, Doc), and those demeanors have nothing to do with you or what you did.

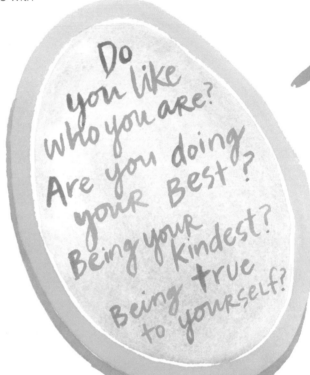

Do you like who you are? Are you doing your Best? Being your kindest? Being true to yourself?

2) Find 3 things in your day to be grateful for

Look at your day from the perspective of gratitude. By proactively searching rather than retrospectively observing, you bring positive energy to all you do. And positive energy attracts good things, good relationships, and good fun. So when your grandma gives you a phone call while you are busy trying to get your homework done, enjoy that special time with her—she sits in a chair all day long because she had a terribly deforming radical mastectomy for breast cancer, but she is alive and so very happy to talk with you. When your soccer team moves you to a different position (one that you aren't happy with), look for how that new perspective fits in with the team and helps you grow.

3) Focus on your CHARACTER STRENGTHS and use those in your relationships and pursuits.

I know the Internet isn't available yet, but a great (free) viacharacter.org survey assesses your strengths and places them in order. Sure, you can feel sad that the lowest five need "self-improvement" (You can't be perfect!), but if you recognize that your top five are "super strong assets," you can use those to your advantage. For example, because you are so compassionate, you might want to become a physician rather than a concert violinist (or you can wait until a hand surgery in your third year of college makes that decision for you.)

4) Practice MINDFULNESS

You don't know it now in the early 1980's, but this world gets super busy, fast, and over stimulating. Instead of that extra twenty minutes of violin practice,

TAKE TWENTY MINUTES EACH DAY TO JUST BE

Get comfortable, focus on your breath, train your mind to refocus to stillness when distractions (like all of your "to do" lists) enter your mind. This will be a PSYCHE-SAVING technique that will help you respond well to stressors, become resilient, and find inner peace (you're from Northern California, after all).

Yes, I know you have too many things to do before each day is all done, but **continue to get good sleep—a rested mind improves efficiency and performance.** And continue to tie your wagon to the farthest star. When your path changes (and it will...several times, drastically), you will be prepared to change course and jump onto another star path.

Love,
Your Forty-Nine-Year-Old Type A-minus Self

TAP INTO YOUR JUNGLE SOUL

BLAKELY STEIN

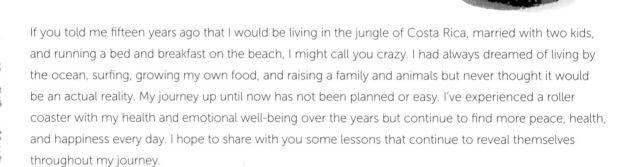

Blakely is the definition of the happy bohemian. She is a passionate foodie, yogini, surfer, and dancer and is living la pura vida, or the simple life, with her husband and children in Costa Rica. Below, Blakely gives you some seriously good advice to live YOUR best life.

If you told me fifteen years ago that I would be living in the jungle of Costa Rica, married with two kids, and running a bed and breakfast on the beach, I might call you crazy. I had always dreamed of living by the ocean, surfing, growing my own food, and raising a family and animals but never thought it would be an actual reality. My journey up until now has not been planned or easy. I've experienced a roller coaster with my health and emotional well-being over the years but continue to find more peace, health, and happiness every day. I hope to share with you some lessons that continue to reveal themselves throughout my journey.

 Doesn't matter how many times you work out, how many kale salads or green smoothies you eat, with stress in your life all of these amazing efforts are canceled. **Stress is the most depleting, acidic, and detrimental emotion to our overall health and wellness.** Find a way to channel your stress, grief, or anger into something positive and amazing. Reinvent or revive a passion or hobby that takes you away from your current reality. If you already have one, get back on it.

CREATE

Whether it be art, dance, writing, or cooking, find a way to channel your creativity into a medium that gives you peace and happiness. Find something that slows you down from your fast, busy lives. Research different groups/organizations in your area to support your creative passion/gift. Create in your home or connect with others in your community.

COMMUNICATION

Be clear with what you want and how you want it. Speak clearly the first time to avoid any conflicts or drama with friends, boyfriends, husbands—speak with intention, integrity, confidence, and grace. Say what you need and how you need it. Open your throat chakra and let it out. The world needs to hear you. What do you have to lose? If they love you, they will stick by your side no matter what. **So put on your big girl pants and express what's not working for you and make the changes you desire.**

HAPPINESS

You can't make everyone happy. Always make time for family and always call your elders, but don't try to fulfill everyone's needs. If you continue to run yourself into the ground, you will live your life being let down. I know because i have suffered from this for many years. When I return from Costa Rica to visit family in the States, I am pulled in many different directions. **Learn to say "No" to people and events that aren't in alignment with your path.** Doing for everyone and nothing for yourself won't help your evolution or happiness.

PRIORITIES

Make to do lists, scratch it out as you go, and rewrite every day. Main priorities at the top. Remember to always make self care/love time for yourself. **When we take care of ourselves, everything else seems to fall in place more easily.**

SELF CARE

Remember to take care of this vehicle you've been given. Nourish, hydrate, and move your body every day. When you give your body love and nourishment, you will be more clear with your thoughts and more driven to accomplish your goals.

WATER

First thing when you wake up, drink water with lemon, as well as before you go to bed and throughout the night. Use a filter, always bring a bottle with you, hydrate as much as possible. Not only is water amazing for your skin and digestion, but it will also flush toxins and bacterias out of your body to prevent getting sick. Increasing my intake of water, herbal teas, and less caffeine has helped my skin and overall health.

 One of the easiest things we can do to improve our health and well-being is to BREATHE. Taking deep, profound breaths in between all acts of living helps move energy around and throughout our bodies. To shift your overall energy and balance in just seconds, try this:

1. Close your eyes.

2. Take a deep breath, in through your nose, using your diaphragm. The breath should go all the way from the tip of your nose down through your belly—inhaling positivity for three seconds.

3. Your breaths should be rhythmic and relaxed, exhaling through your nose for four seconds—releasing negativity, darkness, and all that no longer serves you well.

4. Repeat until you feel as though you have surrounded yourself with a big bubble of bright light.

5. Open your eyes, hold your head high, and always remember to BREATHE.

 Whether you get up from your desk and dance for ten minutes or walk thirty minutes down the road, make sure you move every day. Change it up. Remember your body will continue to change and fluctuate over the years. Don't compare your body to the way it was five years ago or to anyone else for that matter. **Embrace every phase and celebrate your health.**

 Don't pick at your skin, were sunscreen, and wash your face every night and morning with water. Fewer products are better (I used to buy many products and realized that simple is better, less is more). I love washing my face with honey, oats, or ground almonds as an exfoliant and coconut oil as a moisturizer.

Remember to enjoy every phase in life, embrace your body, make time for yourself, move, and be proud of who you are. You have a gift that no one else has, so get out there and share it with the world. You are unique and perfect just the way you are.

ADMIRE YOUR INDIVIDUALITY

LAWANDA RAVOIRA, DPA

Dr. Lawanda Ravoira is a national expert, advocate, author, researcher, and trainer about girls and young women. As the founding President & CEO of the Delores Barr Weaver Policy Center, she works daily to improve the lives of girls who are justice-involved. Her story lets us know that injustices and bias happen too often and in unexpected ways and that keeping a clear sense of self will help us get through them.

Dear Little Lala,

I want you to know that there are times when teachers give us the wrong answers to our questions. In third grade, when you auditioned to play the part of an angel in the Christmas play, you did everything right.

I am proud of how you prepared and learned all of the lines in the play and the words to every song. With fingers crossed and wishes made on the twinkling night stars, you walked on the stage and performed with perfection. You had every right to believe that this would be the year that you were chosen to play the role of one of the angels who would stand on stage in that silver tinseled halo and white flowing gown. You learned from the year before what you could have done better and you were ready! You did your best!

One by one the names of the angels were announced. You were deeply disappointed when your name was not called by your teacher. It took courage for you to ask your teacher why you were not chosen.

I want you to know that the teacher gave you the wrong answer when she said that you were not selected because angels have blonde hair and only the girls with blonde hair could play the role of the angels in the chorus. I know how much you wished that you would wake up and your red hair would magically turn blonde so you could be an angel. In truth, angels come in all sizes, all genders, and have hair every color of the rainbow. Your teacher had been socialized to accept the stereotypes of the popular images of beauty and in doing so, she unintentionally reinforced that beauty myth that teaches girls that they must conform in order to be valuable.

Although I know you were hurt, you still made the bold decision to be part of the Christmas play. I am proud of how you not only accepted but embraced the role of the Christmas tree—and you made it your own! Bejeweled with Mama's costume jewelry that you added to give the cardboard tree more sparkle, you created the most amazing tree ever to take center stage as you proudly announced your one line: "I am the Christmas Tree."

As you grow older, I want you to know that being that unique little cardboard Christmas tree was actually more powerful than being one of the girls who conformed—looking and sounding exactly like the others in order to fit in and be accepted.

JUST LIKE A TREE, IT IS YOUR INDIVIDUALITY THAT WILL BE ADMIRED AND RESPECTED THROUGHOUT YOUR LIFETIME.

It is your uniqueness that will help you to continue to develop strong, deep roots and connections that will enable you to change with the seasons and weather the storms.

With unwavering love,
Your Older Self

PROUD TO BE UNIQUELY YOU!

AKILA RAMAN-VASEGHI

Akila learned early about being a big fish in a little pond. She struggled to accept herself and ultimately learned that her failures were stepping stones to success. Successes like serving on the Board of Trustees for the Cap & Gown Club of Princeton University (her alma mater), becoming a managing director at Goldman Sachs, and as an alumna of W.O.M.E.N. in America, a mentoring group based in New York City.

Dear Teenage Self,

I have some good news for you. We end up having a fabulous life filled with adventure, family, and friends. But we will encounter a few bumps in the road.

When you get out of your small town, it becomes painfully obvious that you are no longer the big fish and you're swimming in a much bigger, more competitive pond. At university, you will encounter people who, like you, were great at many things when they were in high school. The only difference is that some of them are actually THE BEST in their respective fields in the world. Don't let that intimidate you and make you choose a less challenging path. Your confidence and willingness to try new things were your ticket in here, and you too BELONG. You are not an impostor, and every time that thought sneaks into your brain ("Maybe admissions made a mistake!" or **"There weren't many**

other Indian-Korean musician-athlete-students from Missouri to pick from—they HAD to let me in!") please remember that intelligence is diverse, and just because you arrive at an answer differently than someone else doesn't diminish it. In fact, often your answer may be the best one if you don't allow self-doubt to stand in your way of expressing it.

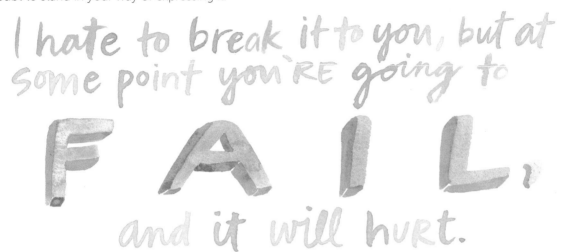

I hate to break it to you, but at some point you're going to FAIL, and it will hurt.

Up until now things have come pretty easily to you, and if you worked hard enough, you've been able to succeed. Straight A's? Pom pom squad? Getting into your top college without applying to a safety school? Check! But you will get your first C. You will bomb an interview. At your first job, you will be told you were the worst starting analyst...ever. **You will learn to quell the welling tears, develop a plan, and pick yourself up. Resilience is a tough skill to learn (you're STILL working at it) but it gets easier over time.** Bouncing back triumphantly will make your "wins" feel even more rewarding.

Now its not all tough lessons today—you will love your career, become more joyful, and you will actually see many of those places you dreamed of visiting (Jungles of Borneo, slopes of the French Alps, shark-infested waters in South Africa, oh my!). You're going to meet a great partner who encourages you to be the best version of yourself and thinks your brilliance is one of your most attractive qualities. And **all those things that make you unique will become a source of pride,** making you memorable to top industry leaders soon enough! Oh, and you will learn to love and appreciate that small town you wanted so badly to escape.

So say thank you to your parents as often as you can (I know, it's hard to fight the eye-roll, but try). Their sacrifices make your life possible, and if you become half the parents they are, you will be a huge success.

Lovingly,
Your thirty-five-year-old self

OVERCOMING THE IMPOSTER SYNDROME

In 1978, two American psychologists, Pauline Clance and Suzanne Imes, coined the term "the impostor syndrome." The impostor syndrome is that feeling of "phoniness in people who believe that they are not intelligent, capable, or creative, despite evidence of high achievement." These individuals "are highly motivated to achieve," yet they "live in fear of being 'found out' or exposed as frauds."

If you ever find yourself feeling like you haven't "really" earned your successes, take a moment and reassess using the steps below.

Acknowledge what you are feeling.

Appreciate your successes! Do not make excuses or call it "luck."

It is OK to be wrong and not know everything.

Trust yourself and fight hard for what you want to accomplish.

GIRL'S GUIDE TO STUDYING

GET ORGANIZED Know what you need to get done and prioritize what you need to accomplish.

25-minute increments are all your brain can handle. **STUDY IN BURSTS**

GET UP Walk around and change locations from time to time to maximize retention of the materials.

Your phone, radio, and TV will offer welcome breaks when you are studying. Leave them off or out of arms reach while you are focused. **LOSE THE DISTRACTIONS**

STAY POSITIVE Believe in yourself and know that you are focused and doing your best work!

— THE MOST — INTERESTING PERSON on EARTH

CARLA JOHNSON

Carla has channeled her love for the environment, geology, and engineering as the CEO and co-founder of EarthVisionz. After traveling across the U.S. to pursue her education, in 1994, she founded Waterstone, Inc., an environmental consulting firm that created and deployed the first 3D virtual earth (before Google Earth)! She believes a deeper connection with the earth can impact social and environmental issues.

Welcome to the biggest group of humans on earth—women! YAY! Our tribe of women live on this planet together and share very similar experiences and feelings at every age, through all stages of life, love, learning, and loss. **Our female bodies are AMAZING, awesome, gorgeous, magical things and inside that body is the most interesting person in the world that you will get to know over and over on a regular basis throughout your whole life.**

And speaking of bodies, make sure you treat it as a temple; it houses you. **Whatever you eat, drink, and breathe becomes part of you, and sometimes it can make you sick.** And forget drugs and junk food, the worst. Imagine if you had just spent hours cleaning your room perfectly and then someone came in and sprayed it with mud, paint, and glue. You would be so mad and exhausted after having to start all over again. What if that happened every day? That's what your body has to do to get rid of the crappola we put in our bodies, it scrubs clean your insides every day. Don't make it have to work so hard. Our pretty little planet earth supplies us already with the cleanest and best things to eat. Don't cave in to fake foods and drinks because they are easy to grab. Read the labels first; if there is no identifiable actual food in it and lots of chemical names, don't eat it. Look for organic labels where you can find it. Non-organic labeled foods can often have lots of chemicals on or in it like pesticides, herbicides, and preservatives to keep thing looking good for months. That's not normal. When you eat well, you feel well.

So here's a little-known secret I learned that I'm sharing with you—the Earth is a living, breathing intelligent being like you. Seriously. It just lives on a whole different time scale. It huffs and puffs and shakes her hips and has lots of friendly and unfriendly creatures living on it (us), and it has a heartbeat too! The center of the earth is made up of liquid iron, spinning like a big gooey blob. Picture buckets of chocolate pudding turning over and over in a dryer. That motion makes the earth spin on its axis and creates a sound like a heartbeat. And the ocean and waters on the land are like its blood, they carry minerals and nutrients to all parts of the planet, giving life and feeding us along the way. The oceans and forests make the air we breathe, so when these things are dirty or have been chopped down, we have less air. Yikes!

THE CHOCOLATE PUDDING

When the planet is not well, we are not well.

Take a moment and think about all that's beneath your feet the next time you walk or stand on the ground. Have a relationship with this slow breathing earth creature. Get to know her and honor her ways of being since, by the way, you are related. You are made up of bits and pieces of her, and she continues to give you life with air, water, food, and shelter. And when her water, air, and soil get polluted with waste and chemicals or the atmosphere gets too hot, she gets kinda sick and stressed out. Did you know that hurricanes are nature's way of getting rid of the heat in ocean? She doesn't mean any harm to us, but when the ocean gets too warm, it hurts the living things in it.

By using your actions, voice, and dollars, I know you can help yourself and the planet feel better.

HERE ARE MY TOP 5 EVERYDAY WAYS TO MAKE THE WORLD A HEALTHIER PLACE:

1) Choose to eat organic when possible. Don't eat anything that the Earth doesn't create. Sustainable gardens and organic farming supports clean soil, water, and food. If you can't get organic, at least eat foods that are made of real plants or animals. And anything you put on your skin is like eating it. It all ends up inside of you and can be harmful or even poisonous over time. (Headaches or stomachaches anyone?)

2) Drink clean water. ALL plastic bottled water is NOT clean water. Plastic leaches into the water and plastic water bottles are one of the biggest sources of pollution killing the oceans. Use a reusable stainless-steel bottle. Get a water filtration unit in your kitchen or for the whole house. Sodas, juices, and other bottled drinks are NOT water. Water is what your body needs to internally clean itself with.

3) Re-think meat. Eat responsibly and less. Know where your meat comes from, Google it. Again, factory meats are full of hormones and chemicals that are not natural. Choose organic, hormone free, and free-range when possible. The oceans are alarmingly overfished to the point of no return for some species, beef is the #1 cause of rainforest deforestation (where lots of the oxygen we breathe comes from) and a chain of other environmental issues, pork and chicken are responsible for much drinking water contamination by nitrates (poop), and a massive amount of agricultural land and crops are sprayed with harmful chemicals.

4) Choose clean energy options. Making and using electricity, gasoline, propane, natural gas, and batteries is a dirty business for the earth. They all create tons of carbon in the atmosphere and harsh chemicals that kill people and the environment. Pay attention people! Turn off lights when you leave a room, drive electric or hybrid cars, opt in for wind or solar power in your communities, walk or ride a bike, recycle, wear a sweater, read about alternative energy. Recycle. Remember, a lot of small actions taken by a large number of people will make a big impact. That's how you and your friends are changing the world for the better.

5) Study your garbage. Holy moly the poor earth is suffering under the weight and toxicity of all the garbage we humans create in the world! Recycle properly and if there is no recycling in your town, work to change that. Consider only buying things with environmentally friendly packaging. Know what you throw out doesn't degrade, it lingers in landfills for hundreds of years, which contaminates the soil and water that people end up eating. Gross. Aim for no more than one bag of garbage per household per week. And stop buying so many clothes and tossing still good ones out. All that manufacturing and shipping and garbage related to clothing is choking the oceans and landfills.

Thank you for listening, the Earth appreciates it and so does every living thing.

Oh, I have one last little tidbit of advice...One day you will look back on the story of your life and it will be like re-reading a book. Every day of your life you are writing a page in your very own biography. I guarantee you will want to like your story. **So be very aware of your choices, have compassion for yourself and learn from your mistakes, continue to get to know the most interesting person on Earth—you—protect and respect your earth home, and you will live a life you love.**

Cheers mate!

IN CLOSING

Each time I have finished reading this book, I am filled with gratitude. Each time, another story fills my heart, gets me thinking, and lets me know that I will truly be OK. **WOW and WISDOM are incredible ingredients for providing us the magical elixir of human spirit and experience that becomes the kind of learning which positively impacts our lives.**

WOWsdom is a community of caring. The goodness that comes from all of us sharing our stories, our knowledge, and being so open is so powerful. **More than a book, WOWsdom is also a place—a community—where we can go to learn from others.** It gave me the chance to take deep breaths and to learn from the paths that others have walked. Ultimately, it provides the insights and support that lets us know that, "It will all be OK," and that, "Yes, I CAN do this," no matter what YOUR "this" is.

This book has been a labor of love, the kind of project that taps your heart and fills your being with passion and purpose. So many people have contributed and to them we should all be grateful; I am eternally so.

To my sister **YaHa, Yvette Angelique Hyater-Adams**, who enthusiastically embraced Generation WOW from day one with her writing, people gifts, and artistic temperament: I am grateful for her guidance, support, and creative gifts that brought Letters to My Younger Self to the stage.

A big thank you to **Shavone Steele,** who immediately embraced Generation WOW with her desire to make a difference in girls' lives. She brought that passion to WOWsdom and, with her fiery enthusiasm, she willed the project into existence with a stellar Kickstarter campaign and the creative flair to move it forward.

We are wowed by the beautiful and inspiring illustrations. Thanks to **Karen Kurycki** who has brought this book to life by reading our imaginative hopes and exceeding each and every one of them. Karen, you are amazingly talented, thanks for elevating all of us.

To the amazing Generation W team: thanks so much to **Kasia Swierczynska**, who is Generation W through and through and a valued advisor all about getting it done and making us better; **Sherry Levin**, who created the meme "It's a book" with her artful video direction; **Patti Minglin, Tara Kelley, Sara Goldsmith,** and **Christina Kostuk** who all believe in contributing to the greater good. Thanks for all your contributions and belief EVERY day. And to **Atiya Abdelmalik,** whose energy will be the life force of what WOWsdom will bring into the lives of girls and women as we build and grow. #gratitude

Thanks to E-V-E-R-Y contributor to this book (you will find their names in our index) for their openness, willingness to share, and their desire to make a difference. I am grateful.

To my "kitchen cabinet," who are always there with a helping hand, an open phone line, a wise word, and enormous hearts—**Jamie Olken, Lisa Shalett, Kelly Madden, Ita Ekpodoum, Christina Norman, Melinda Wolfe, Tina Lifford, Marty Evans, Perrin Rubin, Debbie Banks, Andrea Mail, Larraine Segil, Kelly Watson, Kelly Wallace, Samantha Alves Orender, Audrey Moran, Mary Kellmanson, Cindy Edelman, Amy Ruth, Nina Waters, Susan Townsen, Deirdre O'Grady, Caren Appel, Billie Jo Burr,** and **Shelley Diamond**—there are not enough words to express my gratitude.

Thanks to **Myles Schrag** for being a catalyst and connecting me to our publisher. Thanks also to **Naren Aryal** and **Mascot Books** for believing in this project and to you and your team (hello, **Michelle!**) for investing in it so that WOWsdom! will become the global difference-maker we know it can be.

And to my mentoring friend, **Geraldine Laybourne,** who said to me many years ago, "Do this and I will be there!" She has been there every step of the way as Generation W took shape and continues to evolve all these years later. When we discussed the possibility of a book, her guidance was to create something that was different, that had a distinctive look and feel, and was active and engaging. Gerry, you are magic, and I am ever grateful to you for your friendship and for your forever support of people—women and girls in particular.

A special embrace, of course, to my family: to my husband, **MG,** who has the patience of a saint, and my sons, **Zachary** and **Jacob,** who all provide their support, their insights, and most of all their love. None of this happens without you! xoxoxo

Finally, to you, my WOWsdom friends, this is a beginning, not an end. We will continue to grow and evolve together. Add your stories and lessons to **wowsdom.com** as WOWsdom spreads across the country and the world, bringing with it the lessons that will help us LEARN together and LIVE together, so we LEAD together. THAT will make the world a much better place.

IN GRATITUDE,

Donna

INDEX of CONTRIBUTORS

Be the best **YOU** you can be — no one does **YOU** better than **YOU!**

—CARLA HARRIS

Vice Chairman, Managing Director and Senior Client Advisor at Morgan Stanley, Author, and gospel singer

ABOUT the AUTHOR

Donna Orender was called the most powerful woman in golf while an executive at the PGA TOUR and proudly served as the President of the WNBA, the Women's National Basketball Association. It is here where her passion for helping women and girls coalesced and found its voice in the creation of Generation W. Focusing on the education, inspiration, and connection of women and girls as well as building inclusive communities, her dedication to helping girls achieve their potential earlier in their lives has become a focus of the work of the women of Generation W. A recognized business executive, one of the top executives in sports and top 10 women in sports, she is a game-changer and an outside-the-box thinker. Her philosophy is simple: "Let's do this!"

To learn more about Donna's experience and expertise, please visit Orenderunlimited.com

ABOUT GENERATION WOW

Generation WOW was born from a belief that when women and girls gather, magic happens.
In 2012, seven fantastic young women took the stage at Generation W to share with the 950 women in the audience what was important to them and what they needed to succeed. Magic ensued as Generation WOW was created as that place where girls could learn about the positive and the possible of life. It is a place where the leaders of today would meet with the leaders of tomorrow and create those special relationships that changes lives.

Generation **WOW** believes in ALL girls especially **YOU**

Generation WOW brings together girls of all backgrounds, education levels, and interests—for we know that when we learn to live together and learn together, we will ultimately lead together. Generation WOW focuses on creating the opportunities that help build the future leaders of the world by connecting you to the leaders of today. In the process, girls like you learn how to identify their passions and how to live their purpose. With an emphasis on developing self-confidence, leadership, making connections and smart choices, understanding educational opportunities and the broad breadth of career options, and the power of mentorship, Generation WOW provides you trusted and inspiring experiences that will build your relationships, inspire your dreams, and deliver results that enhance your life. In short, Generation WOW is about making the most of life.

Generation WOW has inspired girls to begin their own WOW clubs in their high schools. **Head to genwownow.org** and learn how you, too, can join in!

YOU DESERVE IT SPEAK your TRUTH PROUD TO BE UNIQUELY

especially with YOURSELF

LIVE, LEARN, LEAD

TOGETHER PRES REGA

OPENING THE DOOR

THINK HAPPY THOUGHTS

AD ASTRA TAKE A

SAFETY MATTERS

BECOMING a WOMAN of INFLUENCE KEEPIN' IT

SAY IT OUT LOUD TO THE UNIVERSE

DEFINE YOURSELF BY YOU STRENGTHS NOT YOUR WEAKNESSES

LIVE, LAUGH, LOVE THROUGH IT ALL

GIVING YOU THE BEST THAT I GOT

START WITH A SMILE

LEARN TO LISTEN AND PRACTICE PATIENCE MONEY DOES MATTE